MW00916012

NEW ZEALAND TRAVEL GUIDE 2025

An Atlas Road Map to Auckland, Wellington, Bay of Islands, Queenstown, Milford Sound, Rotorua, Waitomo, Fiordland National Park, Lake Taupo, Hobbiton, Kaikoura & Wanaka

By

JUDE K. BREMNER

WELCOME TO NEW ZEALAND

(Outer Map of New Zealand)

COPYRIGHT

DISCLAIMER

The information provided in this eBook, **"NEW ZEALAND TRAVEL GUIDE 2025,"** authored by **Jude K. Bremner**, is intended for general informational purposes only. Readers are advised to use the content as a guide.

Legal Compliance

The author and publisher have made efforts to comply with copyright and intellectual property laws. If any inadvertent infringement is identified, it is unintentional, and the author encourages notification for prompt correction.

Conclusion:

"NEW ZEALAND TRAVEL GUIDE 2025," is a tool for inspiration and planning, but it does not substitute personalized travel advice or professional consultation. Readers should exercise prudence and diligence in their travel endeavors.

By using this guide, readers acknowledge and accept the terms of this disclaimer. The author and publisher disclaim any liability for outcomes resulting from the use or interpretation of the information provided herein. **Travel safely and enjoy the wonders of New Zealand with an informed and discerning mindset.**

About The Author

Jude K. Bremner is the person who authored "NEW ZEALAND TRAVEL GUIDE 2025." **Jude** loves exploring different cultures and places, and he wants to share his excitement and knowledge with you through this guide.

A Passionate Traveler:

Jude started traveling to understand the unique stories of each place. He's been to bustling cities and Nations, remote landscapes, and hidden spots, all to discover what makes each destination special.

His Love for New Zealand:

Jude's love for **New Zealand** runs deep. Through multiple visits, he has immersed himself in the region's vibrant neighborhoods and pedaled along its scenic canals. **His encounters shape the authentic insights that make this guide an indispensable companion.**

Master of Insider Tips:

Jude is good at finding hidden gems and authentic experiences. **He wants to share these with you so you can have a memorable trip beyond the usual tourist spots.**

Author's Vision:

Jude's vision with this guide is to help you explore New Zealand like a pro. Exploring **New Zealand** like a pro means to dive into **its culture, history, and vibrant atmosphere,** even without experiencing confusion in the long run or being worried about anything.

Let **Jude** be your reliable companion, unveiling the mysteries of **New Zealand** and ensuring your journey transcends mere travel, transforming into **a truly enriching experience.**

Table of Contents

Bay of Islands
- Historical sites, beaches, and dolphin-watching tours.

Rotorua
- Geothermal attractions, Maori cultural experiences, and the Redwood Forest.

Lake Taupo
- Scenic lake views, Huka Falls, and nearby hiking trails.

Waitomo Caves
- Glowworm caves, Black Water Rafting, and underground adventures.

Hobbiton
- Overview of the movie set tours and surrounding countryside

CHAPTER THREE: The South Island – Majestic Landscapes and Outdoor Escapes

Queenstown
- Adventure sports, Lake Wakatipu, and Remarkables Mountain Range.

Milford Sound and Fiordland National Park
- Boat cruises, scenic flights, and hiking in Fiordland.

Wanaka
- Lake Wanaka, Roy's Peak Track, and local vineyards.

Kaikoura

- Whale watching, seafood specialties, and coastal trails

CHAPTER FOUR: New Zealand's Natural Parks and Outdoor Experiences

Fiordland National Park

- Detailed look at top hiking routes, including the Kepler and Routeburn Tracks.

Tongariro National Park

- Overview of the Tongariro Alpine Crossing and volcanic landscapes.

Abel Tasman National Park

- Coastal walks, kayaking, and marine life.

Mount Cook National Park

- Star-gazing, glacier hikes, and scenic viewpoints.

CHAPTER FIVE: Culture and Cuisine

Maori Culture and Heritage Sites

- Insights into Maori history, art, and local traditions.

Food and Drink

- Traditional Maori food, local wine regions, and must-try dishes.

Festivals and Events

- Major annual events, including Waitangi Day and regional festivals.

CHAPTER SIX: Practical Travel Tips

Accommodation Options

- Overview of hotels, hostels, holiday parks, and unique stays.

Budgeting and Cost-Saving Tips

- Suggestions for affordable travel, food, and activities.

Packing Guide and Health Tips

- Essentials for outdoor travel, climate-specific packing advice, and health tips.

CHAPTER SEVEN: Seven-Day Itinerary for New Zealand

- Day 1: Auckland
- Day 2: Bay of Islands
- Day 3: Rotorua
- Day 4: Waitomo Caves and Hobbiton
- Day 5: Queenstown
- Day 6: Milford Sound
- Day 7: Wanaka

OTHER BOOKS RECOMMENDATION

A KIND GESTURE.

Chapter One: New Zealand Essentials

Overview of New Zealand's unique geography and cultural highlights

New Zealand is a country full of amazing landscapes and rich culture. **It's a very beautiful and magnificent country located in the southwestern Pacific Ocean. This great country is made up of two main islands - North Island and the South Island.** The country also has so many other smaller islands. It's known for its towering mountains, rolling green hills, sandy beaches, and mysterious forests.

Despite its small size, New Zealand's geography is incredibly diverse, and each area of the country has its own character and special sights.

• **The North Island**

The North Island is known for its volcanic landscapes, sparkling beaches, and warm geothermal springs. **There are several active and dormant volcanoes, like Mount Ruapehu and Mount Tongariro, both located in Tongariro National Park.** Some people come to the North Island just to walk the famous Tongariro Alpine Crossing, a hiking trail that takes them past dramatic lava fields, emerald-colored lakes, and views of active volcanoes.

In the central part of the island is Rotorua, known for its bubbling mud pools, hot springs, and geysers. Rotorua sits on top of geothermal fields, and visitors can see steam rising from the ground. This area is also a great place to learn about Maori culture.

Maori are the Indigenous people of New Zealand, and Rotorua is one of the best places to see traditional Maori performances, visit a hangi (a feast cooked in an underground oven), and understand the deep connection Maori have with their land.

At the top of the North Island is the Bay of Islands, a popular destination with over 140 islands surrounded by clear blue water. **The Bay of Islands is famous for its beaches, wildlife, and historic sites.** It's a great spot for activities like fishing, snorkeling, and dolphin watching.

• The South Island

The South Island is often described as a place of breathtaking mountains and calm, blue lakes. The Southern Alps stretch along most of the island, creating a natural border between the east and west. Mount Cook, New Zealand's highest peak, rises sharply in this mountain range, attracting climbers and hikers from around the world. **Near these mountains are large glacier areas, like the Fox and Franz Josef glaciers**, where visitors can explore icy paths or take scenic helicopter rides for an overhead view.

Queenstown, a town on the shores of Lake Wakatipu, is known as the "Adventure Capital" of New Zealand. Here, people can go skiing, bungee jumping, skydiving, and white-water rafting. Queenstown has beautiful scenery and attracts visitors seeking thrills as well as those who want to enjoy its peaceful lake views.

On the southwestern edge of the South Island lies Fiordland National Park, famous for its fiords, deep narrow bays carved by glaciers over millions of years. **The most famous of these is Milford Sound, a fjord with steep cliffs, towering waterfalls, and**

dark, blue water. Many say Milford Sound is one of the most beautiful places in the world.

• **Unique Wildlife and Nature**

New Zealand's isolation in the Pacific Ocean has allowed unique plants and animals to evolve. **New Zealand is home to the kiwi bird**, a small flightless bird with a long beak that has become a symbol of the country.

The kiwi bird is nocturnal and rarely seen in the wild, but you can see it at wildlife sanctuaries. New Zealand is also home to the tuatara, a reptile that dates back to the age of the dinosaurs.

The country is a haven for marine life, too. You can spot dolphins, seals, and even penguins along the coastlines, especially in Kaikoura, where whale-watching tours are very popular.

New Zealanders take great pride in their wildlife and work hard to protect these unique species.

• Maori Culture

The Maori people have lived in New Zealand for over 1,000 years, arriving from Polynesia in long canoes. They have a rich culture that influences many aspects of New Zealand life. **The Maori language, known as Te Reo, is an official language of New**

Zealand, and you'll often see signs and place names in both English and Te Reo.

Maori culture emphasizes respect for the land and natural resources. They believe all things are connected and that every river, mountain, and forest has its own spirit. This connection to nature is called **"kaitiakitanga"** and reflects the Maori role as guardians of the land. Traditional Maori art includes carvings and tattoos (called moko), which tell stories of family heritage and tribal identity.

A famous Maori tradition is the haka, a powerful chant and dance used to express strength and unity. The haka is known worldwide because it's performed by New Zealand's rugby team, the All Blacks, before every match.

• **New Zealand's Modern Culture**

New Zealanders, also called "Kiwis," are known for being friendly, laid-back, and adventurous. Kiwis value the outdoors and often spend their free time hiking, camping, or enjoying the beach. They have a strong sense of community, and you'll find that locals are usually happy to help travelers and share tips on the best places to visit.

New Zealand is also famous for its film industry, thanks in large part to the Lord of the Rings and Hobbit movies, which were filmed across the country. Fans of these films can visit Hobbiton, the movie set village created for the Lord of the Rings series, and other filming locations scattered throughout New Zealand.

Entry requirements, visas, currency, and weather considerations

If you're planning a trip to New Zealand, it's helpful to know about entry requirements, visas, currency, and weather. Getting these basics in order will help make your trip smooth and enjoyable.

• Entry Requirements

To enter New Zealand, you'll need a valid passport. Make sure your passport won't expire within six months after your trip, as some countries require this for visitors. You may also need to show proof of your travel plans, like a return ticket or evidence that you have enough money to support yourself while in New Zealand.

Another requirement is the New Zealand Electronic Travel Authority (NZeTA). Most travelers from countries like the United States, Canada, the UK, and Australia don't need a visa for short stays, but they still need to apply for the NZeTA. You can apply for the NZeTA online or through a mobile app, which is quick and easy. It's valid for up to two years, so if you visit again, you won't need to apply for it a second time within that period.

If you're not from a country that qualifies for the NZeTA, you'll need to apply for a visa before your trip. This visa allows you to visit New Zealand for up to nine months. The most common option for tourists is the Visitor Visa, which you can apply for online.

Be sure to apply early so you have enough time for processing.

• Health and Safety Requirements

New Zealand has strict rules to protect its environment, which means you'll need to declare any food, plants, or animal products you're bringing into the country. New Zealand is very careful about keeping out pests and diseases that could harm their unique plants and animals. Biosecurity officers will check your bags, and you might need to fill out a form to declare any items that could pose a risk.

Because of these strict rules, make sure to clean your hiking boots or camping gear before traveling. Even a small amount of dirt could be flagged, as it might carry seeds or harmful pests.

• Currency and Money Matters

The currency in New Zealand is the New Zealand dollar (NZD), often simply called the "Kiwi dollar." The currency symbol for the New Zealand dollar is "$", and you'll see it written as "NZD" on foreign exchange boards. Notes come in denominations of $5, $10, $20, $50, and $100, while coins include $1 and $2 coins, as well as smaller coins for cents.

Credit cards are widely accepted across New Zealand, especially Visa and Mastercard. Most places accept contactless payments too, which makes things even easier. If you're heading to smaller towns or rural areas, though, it's smart to carry some cash. You can easily find ATMs throughout the country, including in airports, shopping centers, and convenience stores.

Tipping is not as common in New Zealand as it is in some other countries, so don't feel pressured to tip at restaurants. However, it's always appreciated if you want to leave a small tip for excellent service.

• Weather Considerations

New Zealand's weather can vary a lot from one region to another. Because the country stretches from north to south, it covers different climate zones, from subtropical areas in the far north to cooler, temperate zones in the south.

• Seasons in New Zealand

Did you know the seasons in New Zealand are the opposite of those in the Northern Hemisphere? Yes! This means that summer in New Zealand is from December to February, while winter is from June to August. Spring falls from September to November, and autumn is from March to May. Each season offers a different experience for travelers:

- Summer (December - February)

This is the peak tourist season. The weather is warm, with temperatures between 20-30°C (68-86°F). It's a great and perfect time for activities such as hiking, swimming or any outdoor adventure.

- Autumn (March - May)

In autumn, temperatures start to cool down, usually ranging from 10-25°C (50-77°F). It's less crowded, and the landscapes are beautiful with fall colors, especially in the South Island.

- Winter (June - August)

Winter is a good season for skiing and snowboarding. Temperatures are cooler, ranging from 5-15°C (41-59°F). The South Island, especially around Queenstown, gets plenty of snow, making it ideal for winter sports.

- Spring (September - November)

Spring brings mild temperatures between 10-20°C (50-68°F) and blooming flowers. This is an excellent time for outdoor activities like hiking, as it's not too hot or too cold.

• Regional Weather Differences

Because of New Zealand's varied geography, weather can change quickly and can differ greatly across regions. The North Island tends to be warmer and has milder winters than the South Island. Coastal areas, like Auckland and Wellington, usually have more rainfall, while inland areas can be drier.

In the South Island, the west coast receives more rainfall due to the Southern Alps. This creates lush rainforests, but it also means you should be prepared for rain if you're traveling through places like Fiordland National Park. On the eastern side of the mountains, in places like Christchurch, the climate is drier.

The best way to prepare for New Zealand's unpredictable weather is to dress in layers. Bring a rain jacket, even in summer, and keep an extra layer handy if you're heading into the mountains.

• Travel Insurance and Health Tips

New Zealand is known for being a safe place to travel, but it's still wise to have travel insurance. Travel insurance can help cover unexpected expenses like medical bills, trip cancellations, or lost belongings. Healthcare in New Zealand is high quality, but as a visitor, you'll need to pay for medical services if something happens, which can be costly.

If you're planning on doing outdoor activities, like hiking or skiing, look for insurance that covers adventure sports. Make sure to bring any necessary prescription medications with you, along with a copy of your prescription, in case you need more during your stay.

Road trips, public transport, and domestic flights

Getting around New Zealand is exciting because the country offers different ways to travel and see its beautiful sights. You can choose between road trips, public transportation, and domestic flights to reach each part of this scenic country. Let's look at each option to help you decide what might work best for your trip.

• Road Trips

Cars are one of the best ways to get around and see things in New Zealand. With well-maintained roads and beautiful scenery, driving around the country offers a lot of freedom. You can stop wherever you like, explore hidden spots, and enjoy views along the way.

• Renting a Car or Campervan

If you want to take a road trip, renting a car or a campervan is a good option. Rental cars are available at most major airports and in large cities.

Campervans are also popular, especially for those who enjoy camping and want to save money on hotels. You can sleep in the campervan and cook your meals, giving you the flexibility to park near beaches, mountains, or wherever you'd like to explore.

New Zealand's roads are in good condition, but they can be narrow, winding, and hilly, especially in the countryside. If you're renting a vehicle, remember that people drive on the left side of the road in New

Zealand. Speed limits are mostly 50 km/h in towns and 100 km/h on highways, but always watch for signs. Also, keep in mind that roads may be slower in remote areas due to curves and hills.

• Scenic Drives

New Zealand has several famous scenic drives. For example:

- The Pacific Coast Highway

This route on the North Island takes you along the coast, passing stunning beaches, forests, and small towns.

- The Southern Scenic Route

On the South Island, this route covers Fiordland and Southland, showcasing mountains, fjords, and wildlife.

- Arthur's Pass

This route crosses the Southern Alps, offering amazing mountain views.

Before you set out, plan your fuel stops, as gas stations can be few and far between in remote areas. It's also good to check weather conditions, especially in winter when some mountain roads may be snowy or icy.

• Road Safety

New Zealand roads are generally safe, but they can be challenging for drivers not used to hilly or narrow roads. Watch for wildlife, like sheep or deer, especially in rural areas. Always wear your seatbelt, follow speed limits, and avoid using your phone while driving.

• Public Transport

Public transportation is a convenient and budget-friendly option for those who prefer not to drive.

Public transport includes buses, trains, and ferries that connect different regions. While it doesn't reach every remote spot, it covers major cities and popular tourist areas.

• Buses

Buses are one of the most popular ways to travel around New Zealand without a car. InterCity and New Zealand Bus are two main companies that offer long-distance routes. Buses connect large cities like Auckland, Wellington, and Christchurch, as well as smaller towns.

Taking a bus is a good option if you're visiting well-known tourist spots and want to relax while someone else is driving. On a bus, you can look out the window, read, or plan your next destination. Bus tickets are usually affordable, and you can buy them online or at bus stations.

• Trains

Trains in New Zealand are less common than buses, but they provide a special way to see the country. There are a few scenic train routes that show off some of New Zealand's most beautiful landscapes:

- The Northern Explorer

This train travels between Auckland and Wellington, offering views of farmlands, forests, and volcanic landscapes.

- The Coastal Pacific

Running between Picton and Christchurch, this route offers coastal views and passes vineyards, beaches, and mountains.

- The TranzAlpine

Known as one of the world's most scenic train rides, it crosses the Southern Alps from Christchurch to Greymouth.

Train journeys can be more expensive than buses, but they offer a relaxed way to see New Zealand's natural beauty. Some trains even have open-air viewing cars so you can feel the fresh air and take clear photos.

• Ferries

Ferries are essential in New Zealand, especially for traveling between the North and South Islands.

The Interislander and Bluebridge are two companies that operate ferries across the Cook Strait, connecting Wellington on the North Island to Picton on the South Island.

The ferry trip takes about three hours, offering stunning views of the Marlborough Sounds and Wellington Harbour.

Ferries are also useful for reaching islands like Waiheke Island near Auckland, which is popular for its beaches and wineries.

You can take a ferry as a foot passenger, or you can bring your car on some ferries if you plan to drive on the other side.

• Domestic Flights

If you're short on time or traveling long distances, domestic flights are a quick way to get around New Zealand. For example, flying from Auckland to Queenstown is much faster than driving or taking a bus, and it can save you a lot of time.

• Major Airports and Airlines

New Zealand has several major airports in cities like Auckland, Wellington, Christchurch, and Queenstown. There are also smaller regional airports in towns like Rotorua, Nelson, and Invercargill.

The two main airlines for domestic flights are Air New Zealand and Jetstar. Air New Zealand has a larger network and more frequent flights, while Jetstar offers budget options. Both airlines have online booking, and prices vary based on the route and season.

• **Flight Times and Costs**

Flights between major cities usually take one to two hours. For example:

- **Auckland to Wellington**: About 1 hour

- **Christchurch to Queenstown**: About 1 hour

- **Auckland to Queenstown**: About 2 hours

Flying can be more expensive than other forms of transportation, especially during peak tourist season (December to February). However, if you book early, you might find cheaper rates. Some flights are very affordable, especially if you catch a sale or choose a budget airline like Jetstar.

• **Navigating Airports**

New Zealand's airports are generally easy to navigate. Check-in times are shorter for domestic flights compared to international flights, so you won't need to arrive as early.

If you have luggage, most airlines allow one checked bag and one carry-on. Be sure to check baggage policies, as some budget flights may charge extra for checked luggage.

• Choosing the Best Option

Road trips give you the most freedom and allow you to explore at your own pace, while buses and trains let you relax and enjoy the view without worrying about driving. Domestic flights save time for long distances, especially between the North and South Islands.

Many travelers in New Zealand combine different options. For example, you might take a flight to Queenstown, then rent a car to explore the South Island. Or you could use buses and ferries to travel between cities and islands, then walk or use local transport within towns.

Planning your transportation in advance will help you make the most of your time in New Zealand. Each option offers a unique way to see the country, and by choosing what suits your travel style, you'll enjoy a smooth and memorable journey.

Key safety tips for travelers and insights into Maori customs

New Zealand is generally a safe place, and people are friendly and helpful. However, like anywhere, there are basic safety tips and cultural manners that can help you enjoy your visit while respecting others, especially the indigenous Maori people, whose culture has deep roots and unique traditions.

• Safety Tips for Travelers

New Zealand has diverse landscapes, from cities to beaches and mountains, and each setting has its own safety considerations. By following these simple tips, you can stay safe while enjoying everything New Zealand has to offer.

1. Weather Preparedness

New Zealand's weather can be unpredictable. It's possible to have sunshine, rain, and wind all in one day, especially in places like the South Island or mountainous areas. Check the weather forecast regularly, and if you're going hiking or camping, be prepared for sudden changes. Always pack warm clothing, a rain jacket, and sturdy shoes, even in summer.

2. Hiking and Outdoor Safety

New Zealand is famous for its trails and natural beauty, but some areas can be remote and challenging. If you're planning to hike, stick to marked paths, and let someone know your plans. If you're tackling longer hikes, like the Milford Track or Tongariro Crossing, make sure you have enough food, water, and gear. It's also wise to check in with the Department of Conservation (DOC) for trail updates, as some paths may close due to weather or maintenance.

3. Water Safety

New Zealand has beautiful beaches, rivers, and lakes, but water conditions can be risky. Strong currents and unexpected waves, called "rips," can pull swimmers out to sea. If you're not sure about the water, only swim in areas patrolled by lifeguards and follow their instructions. At some beaches, you'll see red and yellow flags—always swim between these flags, as it's the safest area. Never swim alone, and be careful when jumping into rivers or lakes, as there can be hidden rocks or shallow spots.

4. Road Safety

Driving in New Zealand is a great way to see the country, but it's important to stay safe on the road. Remember that New Zealanders drive on the left side of the road, and many rural roads are narrow or winding. Stick to speed limits, and don't rush. If you're feeling tired, take breaks—New

Zealand has many rest stops where you can relax. In winter, some mountain roads may be icy, so drive slowly and carefully. Be mindful of animals like sheep or cows that might wander onto country roads.

5. Wildlife Awareness

New Zealand's wildlife is unique, with many birds, sea animals, and insects you might not see elsewhere. For example, the kea, a native mountain parrot, is known for being curious and sometimes mischievous. While these birds are interesting, avoid feeding them or other wildlife, as human food can harm them. If you're near the sea, keep a respectful distance from seals, penguins, and dolphins. They're amazing to watch, but getting too close can disturb them or be dangerous.

6. Emergency Contacts

In case of an emergency, dial 111. Dialing the number means you're about contacting the fire, police, and ambulance services. New Zealand has a strong emergency response system, and help will come quickly.

However, it's wise to carry a basic first-aid kit, especially if you're traveling in remote areas. New Zealand also has a great search and rescue team, but to prevent needing them, plan your activities carefully and avoid unnecessary risks.

• Insights into Maori Customs

As a visitor, it's respectful to understand some of their customs and be aware of how you can show appreciation for their culture.

1. Understanding the Maori Language

Te Reo Maori, the Maori language, is one of New Zealand's official languages, and you'll see many place names and signs in Maori. Learning a few Maori words or phrases shows respect and can be a fun way to connect with locals. For example:

- **Kia ora:** Hello

- **Whanau**: Family

- **Aroha**: Love

Many New Zealanders, both Maori and non-Maori, will appreciate your efforts to use these words, even if it's just a simple "Kia ora" to greet someone.

2. The Importance of Marae

A marae is a traditional Maori meeting place, often featuring a carved building that represents ancestors and serves as a community center for events and gatherings.

Visitors may be invited to a marae as part of a tour or cultural experience, and it's essential to show respect when visiting.

This includes taking off your shoes before entering, listening carefully to instructions, and following the lead of the Maori hosts.

Usually, there's a ceremony called a powhiri (welcome) that includes speeches, singing, and a hongi, a traditional Maori greeting where people press noses together to share breath.

3. Respect for Sacred Sites and Taonga (Treasures)

Some places in New Zealand are considered sacred, or tapu, by Maori culture. For example, certain mountains, rivers, and lakes hold special significance. In many cases, signs or local guides will tell you if an area is tapu, and it's respectful to avoid disturbing these sites or taking anything from them. For example, when visiting

Mount Taranaki or Cape Reinga, it's polite to tread lightly, take only photos, and avoid loud behavior out of respect.

4. The Hongi and Maori Greetings

When meeting Maori people, you may be invited to participate in a hongi. This traditional greeting involves gently pressing noses and foreheads together, symbolizing the sharing of life and breath. If you're unsure or uncomfortable with the hongi, a warm smile or handshake is usually fine. Maori people appreciate sincerity, so being friendly and genuine goes a long way.

5. Show Respect for Traditional Arts and Crafts

Maori art, such as whakairo (carving), kapa haka (dance), and ta moko (tattooing), plays an important role in expressing cultural identity. These arts are often seen in places like museums, galleries, and cultural centers. Taking photos is usually okay, but it's polite to ask for permission first, especially with tattoos or cultural performances. Avoid imitating or copying Maori tattoos, as they have deep meanings and are not just designs.

6. Haka – A Symbol of Strength and Unity

The haka is a traditional Maori dance that expresses strength, unity, and pride. Many people recognize the haka because it's performed by New Zealand's rugby team, the All Blacks, before games. However, the haka is more than just a performance—it's a way to show respect, passion, and connection. When you watch a haka, enjoy it quietly and respectfully.

7. Giving a Koha (Gift)

In Maori culture, it's customary to give a koha (gift) when visiting a marae or attending a special event. This gift is often a donation to show appreciation. You're not required to bring a koha as a tourist, but if you're invited to a ceremony or event, you might consider giving a small contribution. It's a way to thank the hosts for sharing their culture and traditions.

Chapter Two: The North Island – Culture, Adventure, and Natural Wonders

Skytower, Viaduct Harbour, Auckland Domain, and cultural districts (Auckland)

Auckland, New Zealand's largest city, is packed with interesting sights and activities.

From the towering Skytower that offers breathtaking views, to the lively Viaduct Harbour with its waterfront restaurants, to the peaceful Auckland Domain, there's something for everyone.

Known as the "City of Sails," Auckland is also a hub for culture, art, and history, with neighborhoods and districts that give visitors a taste of New Zealand's diverse culture.

• Skytower

The Skytower is one of Auckland's most famous landmarks, standing at 328 meters tall. It's the tallest structure in the Southern Hemisphere, and it's visible from almost anywhere in the city. Visitors love going up to the Skytower's observation decks, where they can see the whole city and even the surrounding islands. On a clear day, you can see for about 80 kilometers, making it an ideal spot to get your bearings in Auckland and see the city's unique layout with its two harbors and many green spaces.

One of the most exciting parts of visiting the Skytower is the SkyWalk. This is a walk around the edge of the Skytower's main observation deck—without any handrails!

Visitors wear a harness and are guided by trained staff, so it's safe, but it's definitely an activity for those who aren't afraid of heights. For thrill-seekers, there's also the SkyJump, where you can jump from the tower and experience a controlled free fall at 85 kilometers per hour.

If heights aren't your thing, the Skytower also has great restaurants where you can enjoy a meal with stunning views. The Orbit 360° Dining restaurant slowly rotates, giving diners a full view of Auckland while they eat. The Sky Café is another great choice, offering snacks and drinks along with a fantastic view.

• Viaduct Harbour

Viaduct Harbour, located on Auckland's waterfront, is a bustling area known for its restaurants, bars, and marinas. The harbor is home to many yachts and boats, including some that have competed in the famous

America's Cup yacht race. In fact, Auckland has hosted the America's Cup multiple times, and the city takes pride in its sailing culture.

Visitors can take a relaxing stroll along the water, watch the boats, and maybe even book a sailing tour. Several boat companies offer short cruises that give you a view of Auckland from the water and often include snacks or meals. Some tours even let you try your hand at sailing, which is a fun way to experience Auckland's strong connection to the sea.

The area around Viaduct Harbour is lively, especially at night. Many locals and tourists gather here to enjoy dinner or drinks by the water. The variety of restaurants is impressive, with everything from seafood and Italian to Asian fusion and casual pub fare. There's also the New Zealand Maritime Museum nearby, where you can learn about New Zealand's maritime history, from the early Polynesian explorers to the modern-day America's Cup yachts.

• Auckland Domain

Auckland Domain is one of the oldest parks in the city and covers about 75 hectares. Located on the site of an ancient volcano, it's a peaceful place with plenty of space for walking, picnicking, and enjoying nature. The park has beautiful trees, gardens, and wide lawns, making it a perfect spot to relax.

One of the main attractions in Auckland Domain is the Auckland War Memorial Museum. Despite its name, the museum covers much more than just war history. Inside, you'll find exhibits on New Zealand's natural history, including displays of native plants and animals, as well as a section dedicated to Maori culture. The museum has traditional Maori carvings, a meeting house, and a large waka (canoe).

It's a fascinating way to learn about New Zealand's history and culture.

Auckland Domain is also home to the Wintergardens, a lovely spot with glasshouses full of colorful plants and flowers. The Wintergardens are split into two main houses: one is filled with tropical plants, while the other has cool-temperature plants. Outside, there's a large pond with lilies and other water plants. The Wintergardens are open year-round and are free to visit.

If you're lucky, you might also catch one of the concerts or festivals that are held in Auckland Domain throughout the year. Events like the Lantern Festival celebrate Auckland's cultural diversity and bring the park to life with music, food stalls, and colorful decorations.

• Cultural Districts

Auckland is a melting pot of cultures, and its various neighborhoods reflect this diversity. Each district has its own character and is worth exploring if you want to experience the city's art, music, food, and local life.

1. Ponsonby

Ponsonby is known for its trendy vibe, with stylish cafes, boutiques, and art galleries. It's main street, Ponsonby Road, is lined with unique shops selling everything from fashion to home décor. There are also many cafes and restaurants that serve a variety of international cuisines. Ponsonby is especially popular for brunch, and it's a great place to start your day with a good coffee and a delicious meal.

2. Karangahape Road (K' Road)

Karangahape Road, commonly called K' Road, is a lively street with an eclectic mix of art galleries, vintage shops, and music venues.

Known for its creative and bohemian atmosphere, K' Road is a favorite among artists and musicians. You'll find murals and street art decorating many buildings, and there are often art shows and live performances. K' Road is also a top spot for nightlife, with a range of bars and clubs that offer everything from live music to DJ sets.

3. Britomart

Britomart is a stylish area that combines history with modern design. The old buildings have been restored and are now home to high-end shops, cafes, and restaurants.

Britomart is also a transportation hub, with a major train station that makes it easy to reach from other parts of the city.

The area is pedestrian-friendly, and you can enjoy a relaxed stroll around the open square and cobblestone lanes.

Britomart's restaurants offer a mix of local and international dishes, and it's a nice spot to sit outside and people-watch.

4. Parnell

Parnell is Auckland's oldest neighborhood, and it has a charming, historic feel. The area is known for its boutique shops, art galleries, and quaint cafes. One highlight is the Parnell Rose Gardens, which are especially beautiful in spring when the roses are in full bloom. Parnell also has several galleries that feature local artists, making it a great place to see New Zealand's art scene. On weekends, Parnell hosts a farmers' market where you can sample fresh produce, baked goods, and other local treats.

5. Wynyard Quarter

Wynyard Quarter is a newer area on Auckland's waterfront, just a short walk from Viaduct Harbour. It's been redeveloped with modern buildings, open spaces, and playgrounds. The Silo Park is a popular part of Wynyard Quarter, with old silos that have been turned into an open-air cinema and event space. Wynyard Quarter is also known for its waterfront restaurants and food trucks, making it a fun spot for casual dining. Families will enjoy the playgrounds and the interactive water features, which are perfect for kids to splash around in on warm days.

• **The map above shows distance (with time covered) from Wellington to Auckland**

Historical sites, beaches, and dolphin-watching tours (Bay of Islands)

The Bay of Islands is one of New Zealand's most beautiful places, known for its stunning beaches, rich history, and marine life. Located on the North Island, this area is made up of 144 islands scattered across clear blue waters. The Bay of Islands is famous for its historical landmarks, peaceful beaches, and thrilling dolphin-watching tours, making it a fantastic place for anyone who wants to learn about New Zealand's history while enjoying the natural beauty.

• Historical Sites

One of the most important places to visit in the Bay of Islands is Waitangi Treaty Grounds, where a key part of New Zealand's history began. In 1840, British and Maori leaders signed the Treaty of Waitangi here, which helped establish New Zealand as a country. Today, visitors can explore the museum and walk around the grounds to learn more about this historic event. The museum has displays and artifacts that tell the story of the treaty and explain its importance to New Zealand. You can also see a traditional Maori meeting house, called a marae, and a huge war canoe, or waka, which the Maori used in battles.

Another historical spot is Russell, which was New Zealand's first capital. Back in the 1800s, it was a busy port town where sailors, traders, and whalers would gather. Although it was once known as the "Hell Hole of the Pacific" because of the rowdy sailors and rough bars, Russell is now a quiet, charming town with beautiful old buildings and a peaceful atmosphere. Some of the historic buildings in Russell include Christ Church, which is the oldest church in New Zealand, and Pompallier Mission, where early French settlers printed books in the Maori language. Walking through Russell feels like stepping back in time, and it's a great place to imagine what life was like in New Zealand's early days.

Paihia, another town in the Bay of Islands, is also an important place to visit. Known as the gateway to the bay, it's a small town where many travelers start their journey. From Paihia, you can take short ferry rides to nearby places like Russell or to small islands for hiking, swimming, and relaxing. Paihia also has interesting landmarks like St. Paul's Anglican Church, a simple but beautiful wooden church that's been a part of the community since the 1920s.

• **Beaches**

The Bay of Islands is filled with some of the best beaches in New Zealand. These beaches are known for their soft sand, clear water, and relaxed vibe. They are perfect for sunbathing, swimming, snorkeling, or simply enjoying the peaceful views.

One of the most popular beaches in the area is Paihia Beach. This beach is located right in the town of Paihia, making it easy to get to and a fun spot to spend the day. The water is calm and safe for swimming, and there are places where you can rent kayaks or paddleboards. Since it's a popular beach, there are also plenty of nearby cafes and ice cream shops where you can grab a treat.

Long Beach, located near Russell, is another amazing beach with golden sand and clear blue water. It's a bit more secluded, so it's a great spot if you're looking for some quiet time. The beach is long and wide, giving you plenty of space to relax, build sandcastles, or take a stroll along the shore. Long Beach is also known for its beautiful sunsets, which can be breathtaking as the sky fills with shades of orange, pink, and purple.

For those who enjoy exploring underwater life, Otehei Bay on Urupukapuka Island is a fantastic spot. Urupukapuka is the largest island in the Bay of Islands and has beaches with clear waters that are perfect for snorkeling. The marine life here is diverse, and you might see colorful fish, sea stars, and even stingrays if you're lucky. There are also trails around the island, so you can enjoy a mix of beach time and hiking.

• **Dolphin-Watching Tours**

One of the most exciting things to do in the Bay of Islands is to take a dolphin-watching tour. The waters around the islands are home to several types of dolphins, including common dolphins and bottlenose dolphins. These friendly animals are known for their playful behavior, and they often swim right alongside boats, leaping out of the water and putting on a show for visitors.

Dolphin-watching tours usually last a few hours and take you out into the bay on a comfortable boat. The tour guides know where to find the dolphins, and they share information about the dolphins' habits and how they interact with their environment. Sometimes, if the conditions are right, you might even have the chance to swim with the dolphins. Swimming with dolphins is a magical experience, as they are incredibly curious animals and often come close to check out the visitors.

These tours also offer the chance to see other marine life, such as whales, seals, and seabirds. In the winter months, you might spot orcas, also known as killer whales, in the Bay of Islands. The guides on the tours are very respectful of the animals, ensuring that the dolphins and other wildlife are not disturbed or stressed by the boats. The tours follow strict rules to protect the animals, making sure the visits are safe for both the marine life and the people.

Some popular companies that offer dolphin-watching tours in the Bay of Islands are Explore Group and Fullers GreatSights. Both companies have experienced guides and comfortable boats, so you can enjoy the experience fully. Remember to bring sunscreen, a hat, and a camera, as you'll want to capture the moment when the dolphins leap out of the water.

• Island Adventures and Day Trips

The Bay of Islands is not just about the main towns and beaches. With 144 islands, there are plenty of hidden gems and quiet spots to discover. One great way to experience the bay is by taking a day trip to Urupukapuka Island. This island has walking trails, picnic spots, and scenic views, making it a wonderful place for a day of outdoor activities. You can rent kayaks, go snorkeling, or enjoy a quiet lunch overlooking the bay.

Another fun activity is to take a Hole in the Rock tour. The Hole in the Rock is a natural archway on Piercy Island, and boats pass right through it when the weather and waves allow. It's an impressive sight and a highlight for many visitors to the Bay of Islands. If you're lucky, you might see dolphins or other marine life on the way there.

Some visitors also like to visit Cape Brett Lighthouse, which sits on the edge of Cape Brett Peninsula. The lighthouse was built in 1910 and stands tall on a cliff with a stunning view of the ocean. Getting to the lighthouse requires a long hike, but the view is worth it, and you might spot native birds along the trail.

• **The map above shows distance (with time covered) from Auckland to Bay of Islands**

Geothermal attractions, Maori cultural experiences, and the Redwood Forest (Rotorua)

Rotorua, located on New Zealand's North Island, is known for its bubbling mud pools, steaming geysers, and rich Maori culture. This city offers a unique experience with natural wonders, ancient traditions, and a one-of-a-kind forest where giant redwoods grow. Rotorua is a must-visit for anyone curious about geothermal energy, the Maori way of life, and enjoying the outdoors. Let's take a closer look at what makes Rotorua such an exciting place.

• **Geothermal Attractions**

Rotorua sits on a hotbed of geothermal activity, meaning there's a lot going on beneath the ground that creates steaming hot springs, mud pools, and geysers. These attractions are powered by underground heat from the Earth, which pushes hot water and steam up through the ground, creating natural wonders that you can see up close.

One of the most famous geothermal spots in Rotorua is Wai-O-Tapu Thermal Wonderland. This area is like a natural playground filled with colorful pools, bubbling mud, and geysers. The Champagne Pool is a favorite for visitors because of its bright orange edges and turquoise-blue water. It's named the Champagne Pool because of the bubbles that rise to the surface, just like in a glass of champagne. There's also the Devil's Bath, which has a bright green color, caused by minerals in the water. These colors make Wai-O-Tapu a fascinating and beautiful place to explore.

Another incredible spot is Te Puia, where you can see the famous Pohutu Geyser. Pohutu means "big splash" in Maori, and this geyser lives up to its name. It shoots water up to 30 meters (about 100 feet) into the air! Pohutu is one of the largest geysers in the Southern Hemisphere and erupts up to 20 times a day, so there's a good chance you'll see it in action. At Te Puia, you can also see boiling mud pools, which are pools of thick, bubbling mud. They may look unusual, but they show how active the geothermal forces are in Rotorua.

Hot springs are another popular geothermal feature in Rotorua, and some of them are perfect for a relaxing soak. Polynesian Spa is a famous place where you can enjoy hot pools filled with mineral-rich water. The minerals are said to be good for the skin, and the warm water is incredibly soothing. Soaking in a hot spring is a great way to relax after a day of exploring.

• **Maori Cultural Experiences**

Rotorua is a special place to learn about the Maori, the native people of New Zealand.

The Maori have a rich culture with unique art, language, and traditions. Many of these customs are still practiced today, and visitors to Rotorua can experience them firsthand.

One of the best places to experience Maori culture is Tamaki Maori Village. When you arrive, you're greeted with a powhiri, which is a traditional Maori welcome ceremony. This includes singing, dancing, and a speech to welcome you to their land. At Tamaki Maori Village, you'll learn about Maori life, such as how they lived, cooked, and hunted. You can even take part in a haka, the famous Maori war dance known for its strong, powerful movements and chanting. The haka was originally performed by warriors before going into battle, but today it's also performed to show respect or welcome guests.

The Maori people are also known for their traditional hangi feast, which is a meal cooked in the ground. A hangi meal usually includes meat, vegetables, and even dessert, all cooked together in an underground oven. The food is placed on hot stones, covered with clothes, and then buried in the ground to cook slowly.

The result is deliciously tender food with a smoky flavor. At Tamaki Maori Village and other cultural centers, you can taste a hangi meal and see how it's prepared.

Another place to experience Maori culture is Te Puia, which is not only a geothermal park but also a cultural center.

At Te Puia, you can visit the New Zealand Maori Arts and Crafts Institute, where talented artists create beautiful wood carvings and woven items.

These crafts are an important part of Maori culture and often tell stories about the people and their history.

You'll get to see the artists at work and learn about the meanings behind their creations.

• The Redwood Forest

Just a short drive from Rotorua's city center is the Redwood Forest, or Whakarewarewa Forest, a place that feels magical with its towering redwood trees and peaceful atmosphere. This forest is a wonderful place to go walking, biking, or even ziplining, all while surrounded by enormous trees and beautiful scenery.

The redwoods were brought from California to New Zealand over 100 years ago, and they've grown tall and strong in Rotorua's rich soil. The trees here aren't as tall as the famous redwoods in California, but they're still impressive, reaching heights of up to 70 meters (about 230 feet). Walking through the forest, you'll feel small compared to these giant trees. The air is fresh, and there's often a quiet hush, making it a perfect place to enjoy nature.

One of the best ways to experience the Redwood Forest is by walking the Redwoods Treewalk. This is a series of suspension bridges that hang between the trees, allowing you to walk above the forest floor. As you walk from one tree to another, you'll get a bird's-eye view of the forest. At night, the Treewalk becomes even more magical with colorful lanterns lighting up the path, creating a peaceful, glowing atmosphere. The lights don't harm the trees, and they add a gentle glow that makes the forest look like something out of a fairy tale.

The Redwood Forest is also popular for mountain biking. There are trails for all skill levels, so whether you're a beginner or an experienced rider, you can find a trail that's right for you. The paths wind through the trees, sometimes going up and down hills, making it an exciting way to see the forest.

Many visitors say that biking through the Redwood Forest is one of the highlights of their trip to Rotorua.

If you're not into biking, you can enjoy the forest on foot by taking one of the many walking trails. Some trails are short and easy, while others take you deeper into the forest for a longer adventure. You might see native plants and birds along the way, and there are plenty of spots to stop, rest, and take in the views.

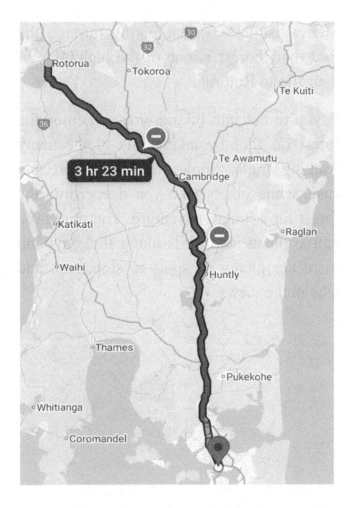

- **The map above shows distance (with time covered) from Auckland to Rotorua**

Scenic lake views, Huka Falls, and nearby hiking trails (Lake Taupo)

• Map of Lake Taupo New Zealand

Lake Taupo is one of the most beautiful places in New Zealand, located in the heart of the North Island. It is the largest lake in the country and offers stunning views, exciting adventures, and plenty of ways to enjoy the great outdoors. Whether you love water activities, hiking, or simply soaking in the breathtaking scenery, Lake Taupo has something for everyone.

• Scenic Lake Views

The first thing you notice about Lake Taupo is its incredible size. The lake is about the same size as Singapore and is surrounded by mountains and forests, creating a stunning backdrop. When the sun shines, the water sparkles like diamonds, and you can see different shades of blue and green depending on the time of day and the weather. Early mornings are especially magical when the lake is calm and mist rises off the water, giving it a peaceful feel.

One of the best places to enjoy the views of Lake Taupo is from Taupo's waterfront.

Here, you can walk along the lakefront, where there are parks and picnic areas. It's a great spot to sit and relax, have a picnic with your family, or just watch the boats glide across the water. The gentle waves make a soft sound, and the fresh air is refreshing.

If you want to see the lake from above, head to the Taupo Lookout. This viewpoint offers a fantastic panoramic view of the lake and the surrounding mountains. It's a perfect place for photos, so make sure to bring your camera! Watching the sunset from here is truly special, as the sky fills with colors like orange, pink, and purple, reflecting off the water.

• Huka Falls

Just a short drive from Lake Taupo is one of New Zealand's most famous natural attractions, Huka Falls. This impressive waterfall is not very tall, but the volume of water rushing over the rocks is truly incredible. The water flows through a narrow canyon and plunges into the Waikato River below with a thunderous roar. The sound of the rushing water is loud, and it's exciting to stand near the edge and feel the spray on your face.

Huka Falls is an excellent spot for families to visit. There are viewing platforms that let you get up close to the waterfall while keeping you safe. You can watch as the water crashes down, and if you're lucky, you might even see a rainbow form in the mist on sunny days. There are also walking paths around the area that lead to different viewpoints, making it easy to find the perfect spot for pictures.

If you want an even closer experience with the falls, you can take a jet boat ride. These fast boats zoom up the river and get you right next to Huka Falls. It's a thrilling adventure, and you'll feel the excitement as the boat speeds through the water. Keep an eye out for birds and wildlife along the way, as the river is home to many different species.

• **Nearby Hiking Trails**

For those who enjoy hiking, Lake Taupo offers many trails that let you soak in the natural beauty of the area. One popular trail is the Lake Taupo Great Walk, a scenic path that runs along the lake's edge. This trail is suitable for walkers of all ages and abilities. You can take a leisurely stroll or challenge yourself with a longer hike. Along the way, you'll see stunning views of the lake, lush forests, and even some volcanic landscapes.

Another fantastic hike is the Tongariro Alpine Crossing, which is a bit further from the lake but well worth the trip. This hike takes you through volcanic landscapes, past steaming craters, and around stunning lakes. It's considered one of the best day hikes in New Zealand. Make sure to pack plenty of water and snacks, as it can be a long trek. The views at the top are breathtaking, making every step worthwhile.

If you prefer a shorter hike, try the Huka Falls Walkway. This trail starts near the falls and takes you along the riverbank, offering beautiful views of the water and surrounding nature. Along the way, you can spot ducks, swans, and other birds enjoying the river.

For a more relaxed experience, consider visiting the Waipahihi Botanical Gardens. This lovely park features various walking trails through beautifully landscaped gardens. You can stroll through the gardens, enjoy the flowers, and even find a spot to sit and take in the scenery. The gardens are also a great place for a picnic, with plenty of shady spots to relax.

Glowworm caves, Black Water Rafting, and underground adventures (Waitomo Caves)

Waitomo Caves is one of the most exciting places to visit in New Zealand. Located on the North Island, this area is famous for its stunning caves filled with glowworms, thrilling underground adventures, and unique activities that make for unforgettable experiences. Whether you're an adventurer looking for a thrill or someone who enjoys the beauty of nature, Waitomo has something for everyone.

• **Glowworm Caves**

One of the biggest attractions in Waitomo is the Glowworm Caves. When you enter these caves, you step into a magical world. The glowworms are tiny creatures that live on the ceilings of the caves. They glow with a beautiful blue-green light, creating a starry sky that looks like something out of a fairy tale.

To see the glowworms, visitors usually take a boat ride through the caves. As you glide quietly along the underground river, the darkness of the cave makes the glowworms stand out even more. It feels like you are floating through a dream. The guides tell stories about the caves, the glowworms, and how they create their light. This is a great way to learn about nature while enjoying a truly beautiful sight.

The cave itself is impressive, with amazing rock formations and waterfalls. Some areas of the cave are very large and open, while others are smaller and cozier. The mix of sizes makes the cave feel interesting and fun to explore.

You might even see stalactites and stalagmites, which are mineral formations that hang from the ceilings or rise from the ground.

• Black Water Rafting

For those looking for a bit more excitement, Black Water Rafting is a thrilling option. This adventure takes place in the same caves but adds a little more action. Participants get to ride on inner tubes through the dark waters of the underground rivers.

To start, you put on a wetsuit to keep you warm in the cool water. Once you're all geared up, a guide takes you into the caves. As you float along, you might find yourself giggling with your friends or family. The ride is filled with twists and turns, and you may even go through some small rapids. It's a fun and safe way to experience the caves up close.

One of the best parts of black water rafting is when you stop for a moment to look at the glowworms. Floating in the dark water and looking up at the glowing lights feels magical. It's a different experience than the boat ride because you're right in the water, surrounded by nature.

After some fun in the water, the tour usually ends with a little hike out of the caves, giving you a chance to see the beauty of the surrounding landscape. The combination of the underground river and the gorgeous scenery makes black water rafting a fantastic adventure.

• Underground Adventures

If you want even more adventure, Waitomo offers various underground activities for all ages. You can choose to go caving, which involves walking, climbing, and sometimes crawling through the caves. This adventure allows you to explore parts of the cave that many visitors don't get to see. It can feel like a mini-expedition as you discover hidden chambers and secret passages.

In these caves, you can also see interesting rock formations and unique wildlife. Some tours even include abseiling, where you lower yourself down into a cave using a rope. It sounds a bit scary, but guides are there to help you every step of the way. This kind of adventure is perfect for those who love to be active and discover new things.

For families with younger kids, there are easier cave tours available that focus on the natural beauty of the caves rather than the extreme adventures. These tours are designed to be fun and educational, teaching kids about the geology and history of the caves in a way that's easy to understand.

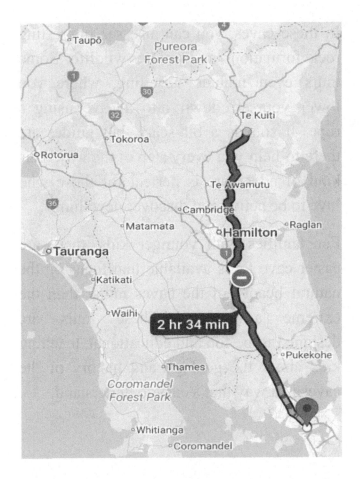

- **The map above shows distance (with time covered) from Auckland to Waitomo Caves**

Overview of the movie set tours and surrounding countryside (Hobbiton)

If you've ever dreamed of visiting a magical place where hobbits live, Hobbiton is the perfect destination for you. Located in New Zealand's North Island, this famous movie set brings to life the enchanting world of J.R.R. Tolkien's special known as 'The Lord of the Rings' & 'The Hobbit.' When you visit Hobbiton, you not only get to see the movie set but also enjoy the beautiful countryside that surrounds it.

• The Hobbiton Movie Set

Hobbiton is a charming movie set designed to look like the home of hobbits, who are small, friendly people with big hearts. The set is full of colorful hobbit holes, gardens, and rolling green hills. As soon as you arrive, you can feel the magic in the air. The best way to see Hobbiton is by joining a guided tour. These tours last about two hours and take you through the entire movie set.

During the tour, your guide will share interesting stories about how the films were made and what it was like to work with the actors. You'll learn fun facts about the hobbits, like how they love to eat and enjoy a good party. The guides are usually very knowledgeable and can answer any questions you might have.

As you walk through the set, you'll see the famous hobbit holes, each with its unique look. Some have cute little doors and windows, while others have lovely gardens full of flowers and vegetables. You can also visit places like the Green Dragon Inn, where hobbits enjoy a drink, and the Party Tree, which is a favorite spot for celebrations. Every corner of Hobbiton is filled with details that make it feel real, from the tiny smoke rising from the chimneys to the sound of birds singing in the trees.

• The Surrounding Countryside

The beauty of Hobbiton isn't just in the movie set itself; it's also in the stunning countryside around it. The area is filled with lush green fields, rolling hills, and beautiful trees. As you walk around Hobbiton, you can take in the fresh air and enjoy the sounds of nature.

The landscape is perfect for taking pictures, so don't forget to bring your camera! You can capture the vibrant colors of the flowers, the deep blue sky, and the bright green grass. The views are especially lovely on sunny days, when everything seems to sparkle.

• Special Features

In addition to the regular tours, Hobbiton offers some special experiences. One of the most popular is the evening tour, where visitors can see Hobbiton lit up with lanterns and fairy lights. The atmosphere changes completely at night, and it feels magical to wander through the set when it's dark outside. You might even enjoy a drink and a meal at the Green Dragon Inn, making it a truly unforgettable experience.

For those who love nature, there are also walking trails around the countryside. These trails let you explore the beautiful landscape at your own pace. You can spot different kinds of plants and animals along the way. The fresh air and peaceful environment make it a great way to spend time outdoors.

• Learning Opportunities

Hobbiton is not just about fun and games; it also provides a chance to learn. Many visitors enjoy hearing about the hard work that went into creating the movie set. The designers, builders, and artists put a lot of effort into making Hobbiton look perfect for the films. Learning about the process can inspire young visitors to be creative and think about what goes into making movies.

Additionally, Hobbiton is a place where you can learn about New Zealand's farming and agricultural practices. The surrounding countryside has a rich farming history, and you can often see sheep and other farm animals grazing in the fields. The guides may talk about the importance of farming in New Zealand and how it connects to the culture and economy.

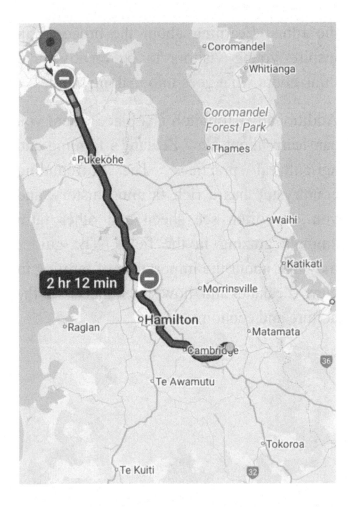

- **The map above shows distance (with time covered) from Auckland to Hobbiton**

Chapter Three: The South Island – Majestic Landscapes and Outdoor Escapes

Adventure sports, Lake Wakatipu, and Remarkables Mountain Range (Queenstown)

Queenstown is often called the adventure capital of New Zealand, and it's easy to see why. This beautiful town is surrounded by stunning landscapes, including the sparkling waters of Lake Wakatipu and the impressive Remarkables Mountain Range. If you love outdoor activities, Queenstown is the perfect place for you.

• Adventure Sports

In Queenstown, there is no shortage of adventure sports for everyone to enjoy. Whether you're looking for something thrilling or just a fun way to spend the day, you'll find it here. An activity famous in this place is bungee jumping. Imagine jumping off a bridge high above a river, with the wind rushing past you and the ground far below. It's a heart-pounding experience that many people come to Queenstown just to try. If you're feeling brave, you can take a leap off the Kawarau Bridge, where the first commercial bungee jump took place.

If jumping isn't your style, you might enjoy skydiving. You can soar through the air and enjoy incredible views of Lake Wakatipu and the mountains below as you free-fall from a plane. Once your parachute opens, you'll float gently back to the ground, feeling like you're on top of the world.

Queenstown also offers plenty of activities on the water. You can try jet boating, which is an exciting ride in a fast boat that can spin and slide across the water. The drivers are skilled at navigating through narrow canyons and will give you an unforgettable ride. Another great water activity is kayaking. You can paddle around Lake Wakatipu and take in the beautiful scenery at your own pace.

For those who prefer being on land, Queenstown has plenty of hiking and biking trails. There are paths for everyone, from easy walks along the lake to challenging hikes in the mountains. The views from the top are worth every step, and you'll feel great after spending time outdoors.

• Lake Wakatipu

Lake Wakatipu is a stunning lake that is shaped like a zigzag. It is one of the largest lakes in New Zealand and is known for its clear blue waters. The lake is surrounded by majestic mountains, making it a picture-perfect location for both relaxation and adventure.

One of the best ways to enjoy Lake Wakatipu is by taking a boat cruise. Several companies offer trips on the lake, where you can sit back, relax, and take in the incredible scenery.

On a sunny day, the water sparkles like diamonds, and the mountains stand tall against the bright blue sky.

Some cruises even provide opportunities to see wildlife, such as birds and sometimes even seals.

If you're feeling more active, you can try swimming in the lake. The water can be cold, but on a warm day, it's refreshing and fun.

You can also bring a picnic and find a nice spot by the lake to enjoy lunch while taking in the view.

• Remarkables Mountain Range

The Remarkables Mountain Range is a beautiful backdrop to Queenstown. The mountains are steep and dramatic, with rugged peaks that seem to touch the sky. They are especially stunning in winter when the tops are covered in snow. The Remarkables are home to many outdoor activities, making them a great place to visit all year round.

It's a ski destination. There are ski slopes for all levels, from beginners to advanced skiers. You can take lessons if you're new to skiing or snowboarding, so everyone can join in the fun. Gliding down the slopes with the crisp mountain air on your face is an experience you won't forget.

In the summer, the Remarkables offer excellent hiking trails. You can explore the mountains on foot, with paths that lead to breathtaking views. Some trails take you to hidden lakes or give you a chance to see unique plants and animals. It's a great way to feel connected to nature and see the beauty of New Zealand.

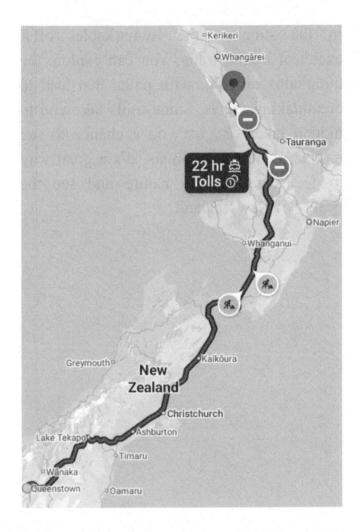

• The map above shows distance (with time covered) from Auckland to Queenstown

Boat cruises, scenic flights, and hiking in Fiordland (Milford Sound and Fiordland National Park)

Fiordland National Park is home to the famous Milford Sound, which is known for its dramatic scenery, including towering cliffs, lush rainforests, and beautiful waterfalls. Many people come to Fiordland to see its natural wonders, and there are three great ways to experience this amazing area: boat cruises, scenic flights, and hiking.

• Boat Cruises

One of the best ways to see Milford Sound is by taking a boat cruise. There are many companies that offer cruises on the sound, and they usually last about one to two hours.

As you set off on the water, you will quickly be amazed by the tall cliffs that rise steeply from the water. These cliffs are often covered in green vegetation, which creates a stunning contrast against the blue waters of the sound.

During the cruise, you can spot beautiful waterfalls cascading down the cliffs. One of the most famous waterfalls is called Stirling Falls.

When the boat gets close, you can feel the mist from the falls on your face, which is a refreshing treat, especially on a sunny day. You might even see rainbows in the mist, adding to the magic of the place.

The boat trips often include a knowledgeable guide who shares interesting facts about the area. You will learn about the history, geology, and wildlife of Fiordland.

Keep your eyes open, as you might see playful dolphins swimming alongside the boat or seals lounging on the rocks. With every turn of the boat, you will find new views that take your breath away.

• Scenic Flights

If you want a different perspective of Fiordland, consider taking a scenic flight. This is a wonderful way to see the park from above. You can choose between helicopter rides and small airplane flights. Either option offers fantastic views of the stunning landscapes below.

As you fly over Milford Sound, you will see the cliffs and waterfalls from a bird's-eye view. The sight of the sound from the sky is something special. You may also spot the many fjords that make up the area, including dramatic peaks and hidden lakes. The colors of the water and the land are even more vibrant from above.

Many flights also include landings on the mountains or nearby glaciers, giving you a chance to step out and experience the beauty up close. It's a thrilling experience to land in such remote and stunning locations. Just remember to take your camera to capture the amazing sights!

• Hiking in Fiordland

For those who enjoy being on foot, Fiordland has some of the best hiking trails in New Zealand. There are many different walks to choose from, ranging from easy strolls to challenging hikes. No matter your skill level, you can find a trail that suits you.

In Fiordland, a famous hike is the Milford Track. It is often called the **"finest walk in the world."** This multi-day hike takes you through lush forests, past beautiful rivers, and up to incredible mountain views. Along the way, you will encounter a variety of wildlife, including unique birds like the kea, a playful alpine parrot. Many people choose to hike the Milford Track as part of a guided tour, which allows you to fully enjoy the scenery without worrying about navigation.

If you prefer a shorter hike, there are many day walks around Milford Sound as well. The Routeburn Track is another fantastic option, offering a glimpse of the stunning landscapes without the commitment of a multi-day trek. Shorter walks lead to viewpoints that overlook the sound and its beautiful surroundings.

When hiking in Fiordland, it's important to remember a few key things. The weather can change quickly, so it's best to be prepared for rain or shine. Wear sturdy shoes and bring water, snacks, and a camera to capture the unforgettable views. Taking your time on the trails allows you to fully enjoy the natural beauty and listen to the sounds of nature around you.

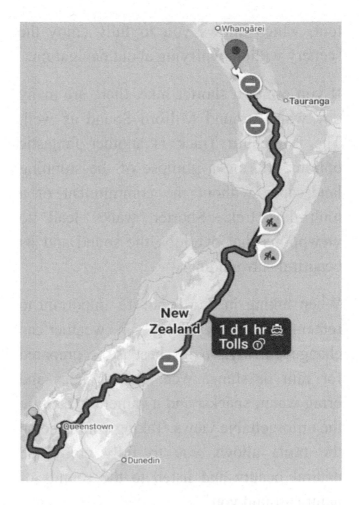

• The map above shows distance (with time covered) from Auckland to Milford Sound

• **The map above shows distance (with time covered) from Auckland to Fiordland National Park**

Lake Wanaka, Roy's Peak Track, and local vineyards (Wanaka)

Wanaka is a charming town located in the southern part of New Zealand's South Island. It sits beside the stunning Lake Wanaka, which is known for its crystal-clear waters and beautiful scenery. This area is a perfect place for outdoor adventures, relaxation, and enjoying some delicious local food and drink. Let's take a closer look at Lake Wanaka, the famous Roy's Peak Track, and the delightful vineyards that make this region so special.

• Lake Wanaka

Lake Wanaka is one of New Zealand's largest lakes, and it offers breathtaking views all year round. The lake is surrounded by mountains, which make it a perfect spot for taking pictures.

Many people come to the lake to enjoy various activities. In the summer, you can swim, kayak, or paddleboard on the calm waters.

The clear blue lake feels refreshing on a hot day, and you can often see fish swimming below the surface.

If you enjoy fishing, Lake Wanaka is also a great place to cast a line.

Trout are common in the lake, and fishing can be a fun way to spend the day. Just remember to check the local fishing rules before you start!

In the winter, the area around the lake transforms into a winter wonderland. The nearby mountains are perfect for skiing and snowboarding.

People travel from all over to enjoy the snowy slopes. After a day on the mountain, it's nice to relax by the lake and watch the sunset paint the sky in beautiful colors.

• Roy's Peak Track

One of the best things to do in Wanaka is hike the Roy's Peak Track. This trail is very popular because it offers some of the most amazing views in New Zealand. The hike takes you to the top of Roy's Peak, which stands at 1,578 meters (5,177 feet) above sea level. It's not an easy hike, but the journey is worth it!

The trail begins at a parking area about a 10-minute drive from Wanaka. As you start your hike, you will walk through fields with sheep and other farm animals. The path gradually climbs higher, and you can see the beautiful lake and mountains in the distance. Along the way, there are plenty of places to stop and catch your breath while taking in the scenery.

As you get closer to the top, the views become more spectacular. You can see Lake Wanaka stretching out below, with its deep blue waters shimmering in the sunlight. On a clear day, you can even see Mount Aspiring and the surrounding peaks, creating a stunning backdrop.

When you finally reach the summit, it feels like you're on top of the world. You can take photos and enjoy a well-deserved snack while looking at the incredible landscape around you. Remember to bring plenty of water and wear good hiking shoes, as the trail can be steep and rocky.

• **Local Vineyards**

Another great reason to visit Wanaka is its local vineyards. The region is known for producing excellent wines, particularly pinot noir and riesling. The vineyards are located on the rolling hills surrounding Lake

Wanaka, and visiting them is a delightful way to spend an afternoon.

Many vineyards offer tours and tastings, where you can learn about how wine is made and sample some of the delicious varieties they produce. The staff are usually very friendly and happy to share their knowledge about wine. You can also find lovely restaurants at the vineyards that serve delicious meals made with fresh, local ingredients. Enjoying a meal with a view of the vineyards and mountains is a treat!

If you're with family or friends, a vineyard visit can be a fun experience. Some places even have picnic areas where you can relax and enjoy a meal outdoors. It's a nice way to spend time together while soaking up the beauty of the area.

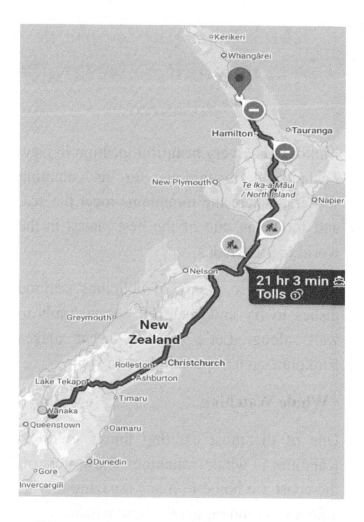

• **The map above shows distance (with time covered) from Auckland to Wanaka**

Whale watching, seafood specialties, and coastal trails (Kaikoura)

Kaikoura is a very beautiful location in New Zealand. It is famous for its stunning scenery, where the mountains meet the sea, and for being one of the best places in the world to see whales.

There are also plenty of delicious seafood dishes to try and beautiful coastal trails to walk along. Let's discover what makes Kaikoura such a special place to visit.

• Whale Watching

One of the most exciting things to do in Kaikoura is whale watching. The waters off the coast are home to many amazing marine animals, including giant sperm whales.

These whales can grow to be as long as a school bus and can dive deep into the ocean to hunt for food. When they come up for air, you can see their big tails splashing in the water.

There are several tour companies in Kaikoura that offer whale watching trips.

You can choose to go on a boat or even take a scenic flight to see the whales from the air. On a boat, you might be able to spot not just sperm whales, but also dolphins and seals playing in the waves.

Many people find it thrilling to see these animals in their natural habitat. The guides on these tours know a lot about the whales and will share interesting facts with you during the trip.

Whale watching is best during certain times of the year, so it's a good idea to check when the whales are most active.

Regardless of when you visit, there's a good chance you'll have a memorable experience seeing these magnificent creatures.

• Seafood Specialties

After an exciting day of whale watching, it's time to enjoy some of Kaikoura's famous seafood. Because the town is right by the ocean, it is known for its fresh fish and shellfish. You can find many restaurants and cafes that serve delicious dishes made from locally caught seafood.

One of the most popular dishes is crayfish, also known as rock lobster. It's a special treat in Kaikoura and is often cooked simply to let the fresh flavors shine. Many visitors enjoy eating crayfish straight from the shell with a bit of lemon juice. You can also find fish and chips at local takeaways, where you can enjoy crispy fish served with golden fries. Eating fresh seafood while looking out at the ocean is a delightful experience.

Some places even offer guided seafood tours, where you can learn how to catch and cook your own fish. This can be a fun and educational activity for families and friends. You might even get to try your hand at fishing for your dinner!

• Coastal Trails

Kaikoura is also known for its beautiful coastal trails. These walking paths offer stunning views of the ocean, mountains, and wildlife. One of the most popular trails is the Kaikoura Peninsula Walkway, which takes you along the coastline. This trail is easy to walk and is suitable for people of all ages.

As you walk, you might see seals lounging on the rocks and birds flying overhead. Keep your eyes peeled for dolphins swimming in the water, especially if you visit during the warmer months. The sound of the waves crashing against the shore creates a peaceful atmosphere as you take in the beauty of nature.

The trail has several lookout points where you can stop and take pictures. At some points, you'll be able to see the snow-capped mountains rising in the background, making for a stunning view. There are also picnic spots where you can rest and enjoy a snack while taking in the scenery.

If you're feeling adventurous, you can also explore some of the more challenging trails in the area, like the Mount Fyffe Track. This hike leads you up into the mountains and offers breathtaking views of the coastline and the surrounding landscape.

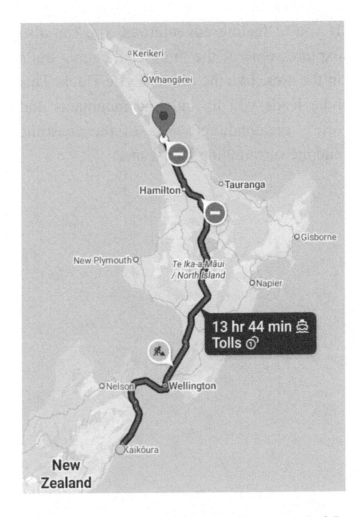

- **The map above shows distance (with time covered) from Auckland to Kaikoura**

Chapter Four: New Zealand's Natural Parks and Outdoor Experiences

Detailed look at top hiking routes, including the Kepler and Routeburn Tracks (Fiordland National Park)

Fiordland National Park is known for its deep valleys, stunning lakes, and towering mountains. It's also home to some of the world's best hiking trails. Two of the most popular routes here are the Kepler Track and the Routeburn Track. These trails allow hikers to explore the incredible landscapes of Fiordland and see its unique plants, animals, and beautiful views up close. Let's take a closer look at what each of these amazing tracks has to offer and what makes them special.

• **Kepler Track**

The Kepler Track is a 60-kilometer loop that begins and ends near the town of Te Anau. This track was built to show off Fiordland's different landscapes, from lush forests to alpine mountain tops. Unlike some other tracks in New Zealand, the Kepler Track was specifically designed for hiking, so it takes you through a variety of environments in a relatively short distance.

The entire hike usually takes about three to four days, with huts available along the way where hikers can rest overnight. Here's a breakdown of what you'll see along the Kepler Track:

Day 1: Luxmore Hut

The journey typically starts at the Control Gates near Lake Te Anau. From there, hikers head through peaceful beech forests where tall trees and bird songs create a welcoming atmosphere. After a few hours, the trail starts to climb, and soon you'll reach the alpine area. Here, the views start to open up, showing Lake Te Anau and the surrounding valleys. The first night is usually spent at Luxmore Hut, a high-altitude hut with breathtaking views.

Day 2: Iris Burn Hut

On the second day, hikers move from Luxmore Hut across alpine ridges. This part of the trail is considered one of the highlights because of the panoramic views of Fiordland's mountains and valleys.

The trail continues along the ridge before descending into the forested Iris Burn Valley. Here, hikers often spot native birds and sometimes even a friendly kea, a New Zealand alpine parrot known for its curious nature. The night is usually spent at Iris Burn Hut.

Day 3: Moturau Hut

The third day is more relaxed, as the trail descends further through the forest, leading hikers to the shores of Lake Manapouri. The forest here is dense and rich with ferns, mosses, and birdlife. Moturau Hut sits near the lake, offering a peaceful setting for the night.

Day 4: Return to Control Gates

The final day is a shorter walk along easy forest paths, leading back to the starting point. This section of the trail is gentle, giving hikers a chance to enjoy the sounds of nature and reflect on the journey.

• Routeburn Track

The Routeburn Track is another famous trail in Fiordland, stretching 33 kilometers from the Divide, near Milford Sound, to the

Routeburn Shelter, near Glenorchy. It typically takes two to three days to complete and crosses over into the neighboring Mount Aspiring National Park. The Routeburn Track offers a variety of landscapes, from beech forests to mountain passes, and is a shorter but equally stunning alternative to longer tracks.

Here's a closer look at what you'll experience on the Routeburn Track:

Day 1: Routeburn Flats Hut or Routeburn Falls Hut

Most hikers start at the Routeburn Shelter and follow the trail through thick forests of beech trees. The sound of flowing streams and native birds creates a calm environment as you walk. After a few hours, the trail reaches Routeburn Flats, an open area with views of the surrounding mountains. Some hikers choose to stay at the Routeburn Flats Hut, but many continue a bit further to the

Routeburn Falls Hut, which sits higher up and offers amazing views of Routeburn Valley.

Day 2: Harris Saddle and Lake Mackenzie Hut

On the second day, hikers climb to Harris Saddle, the highest point on the Routeburn Track. This section is one of the most impressive, as it offers wide views of Fiordland's rugged terrain. Along the way, hikers pass Lake Harris, a beautiful alpine lake. After crossing Harris Saddle, the trail descends through a valley to Lake Mackenzie Hut, where hikers can rest for the night.

Day 3: The Divide

The final day of the Routeburn Track takes hikers through a section of lush forest and across the Earland Falls, a beautiful waterfall where hikers often stop to take photos. From here, it's a steady descent to the Divide, where the trail ends.

The Divide is close to Milford Sound, making it easy for hikers to continue their journey to this iconic destination.

- **Tips for Hiking the Kepler and Routeburn Tracks**

1. Book Huts in Advance

Hikers need to book huts on both the Kepler and Routeburn Tracks through the Department of Conservation (DOC) website. These huts fill up quickly, especially during the summer season (December to February), so early booking is essential.

2. Pack for All Weather

Fiordland weather can be unpredictable. Even in summer, it's common to experience rain, wind, and chilly temperatures. It's essential to bring layers, including a waterproof jacket, warm clothing, and sun protection.

3. Carry Sufficient Food

While huts provide basic shelter and a place to sleep, they don't offer food, so hikers must carry enough food for the entire hike. Lightweight and high-energy snacks, such as nuts, dried fruit, and energy bars, are good choices.

4. Respect Nature and Leave No Trace

Fiordland National Park is a protected area with fragile ecosystems. Hikers are encouraged to follow the Leave No Trace principles, which means carrying out all trash, staying on marked trails, and respecting wildlife.

5. Stay Safe on the Trails

It's important to be mindful of the environment and know your limits. Weather can change rapidly in Fiordland, so always check the forecast and listen to any advice from DOC staff before starting.

• Why Hike in Fiordland?

The Kepler and Routeburn Tracks showcase some of the best that Fiordland has to offer, from sweeping mountain views to peaceful forests. These trails give hikers a chance to experience New Zealand's wild beauty and encounter unique wildlife in their natural habitats.

Hiking the Kepler and Routeburn Tracks is an adventure that combines physical activity with nature appreciation. The beauty, serenity, and sense of accomplishment you'll feel when walking these trails are unforgettable. For anyone looking to experience the wonders of Fiordland National Park, these hikes are a must-try.

Overview of the Tongariro Alpine Crossing and volcanic landscapes (Tongariro National Park)

Tongariro National Park holds a special place in both natural and cultural history. Located in the central North Island, this park is home to towering volcanoes, unusual rock formations, bright blue lakes, and rugged terrain that looks like something out of a fantasy world. One of the most famous parts of the park is the Tongariro Alpine Crossing, a day hike that's known as one of the best hikes in New Zealand and even the world.

The Tongariro Alpine Crossing takes hikers right through the heart of this volcanic landscape. It's a challenging hike that lets you see some of the most unique sights in the park, from ancient lava flows to steaming craters and colorful lakes. Here's what makes this hike special, what to expect, and some important tips for those planning to go.

- **Overview of the Tongariro Alpine Crossing**

The Tongariro Alpine Crossing is a 19.4-kilometer (about 12 miles) hike that typically takes about 6 to 8 hours to complete. This is not a loop, so hikers start at one end and finish at the other. The track climbs through volcanic terrain, reaching high points where you can see amazing views of the park and its famous volcanoes: Mount Tongariro, Mount Ngauruhoe, and Mount Ruapehu. Mount Ngauruhoe, known as "Mount Doom" in the Lord of the Rings movies, is especially recognizable.

The hike passes through a variety of landscapes, including barren fields, steep slopes, and alpine meadows. It's like walking on a different planet because of the dark rocks, volcanic vents, and bright colors of the lakes. The trek is challenging because of the distance and some steep sections, but the rewards along the way make it worth the effort.

• **Key Highlights of the Tongariro Alpine Crossing**

1. Mangatepopo Valley

The hike starts at Mangatepopo Car Park, where you enter the Mangatepopo Valley. This area is gentle and easy to walk through, surrounded by low vegetation and rocks left from past eruptions.

As you walk through the valley, you'll see Mount Ngauruhoe in the distance, standing tall and impressive.

2. Soda Springs

After some time, the trail passes Soda Springs, a small waterfall with fresh water coming from the mountains.

This spot is a good place to take a break and prepare for the next part of the hike, as the trail gets steeper from here.

3. The Devil's Staircase

The Devil's Staircase is one of the toughest parts of the crossing. It's a steep climb up a series of rocky steps, taking hikers higher into the mountains.

Although it's challenging, reaching the top brings a great sense of accomplishment and offers views that are worth the effort.

4. South Crater

After the Devil's Staircase, you reach the South Crater, a large flat area that's covered in dark sand and volcanic rocks.

This crater feels wide open and empty, like a desert on the moon.

Walking across it is relatively easy, and it gives you a break before the next uphill section.

5. Red Crater

Climbing up to Red Crater is another challenging part of the hike, but it's one of the most memorable. The Red Crater is named for its deep red color, caused by minerals in the volcanic rock. This area sometimes has steam coming out of vents, reminding you that the volcano is still active. The view from here is incredible, with the surrounding mountains and craters stretching out in all directions.

6. Emerald Lakes

One of the most popular spots on the Tongariro Alpine Crossing is the Emerald Lakes. These are three small, bright green lakes that sit in the middle of the volcanic landscape. The color comes from minerals in the water, and they look striking against the dark rocks around them. This is a great spot for photos, and many hikers take a break here to enjoy the view.

7. Blue Lake

Not far from the Emerald Lakes is the Blue Lake, a large, peaceful lake with a striking blue color. The water in this lake is very pure, and in Maori tradition, it's a sacred place, so visitors are asked not to swim in it. The Blue Lake is calm and reflective, providing a sense of peace after the excitement of the steep climbs.

8. Descent to Ketetahi Hut

After the Blue Lake, the track begins to descend, winding its way down towards Ketetahi Hut. The views here change from alpine to grassy slopes, with small shrubs and wildflowers. The path eventually leads into a forested area, offering shade and a cooler environment for the last part of the hike.

9. End at Ketetahi Car Park

The track finishes at Ketetahi Car Park. Here, you'll likely feel tired but proud, with a sense of achievement after completing one of New Zealand's most famous hikes.

• The Volcanic Landscape of Tongariro

Tongariro National Park is a UNESCO World Heritage site because of its unique volcanic landscape and cultural significance to the Maori people. The park includes three major volcanoes: Tongariro, Ngauruhoe, and Ruapehu. These volcanoes are still active, and eruptions have shaped the land over thousands of years.

The volcanic features make this area unlike any other. The dark rocks, red craters, and steam vents give the park an intense and rugged appearance.

The area also has strong cultural connections for the Maori people, who have lived here for centuries and regard the mountains as sacred.

The volcanoes and craters are connected to Maori legends and traditions, and the land is carefully protected.

• Insights for Hiking this Alpine Crossing successfully

1. Plan for the Weather

In Tongariro National Park, the weather is not usually constant. It's important to check the forecast before you go and be prepared for sudden changes. Even in summer, temperatures can drop, and it may rain or even snow. Bring warm layers, a waterproof jacket, and sturdy shoes.

2. Start Early

The Tongariro Alpine Crossing is a long hike, so it's best to start early in the morning to have plenty of daylight. It can get busy, so starting early also helps you avoid the crowds and lets you take your time.

3. Bring Plenty of Food and Water

There are no shops or water fountains along the way, so make sure you carry enough food and water for the entire hike. High-energy snacks like nuts, fruit, and energy bars are a good idea, and bring at least two liters of water.

4. Respect the Environment

Tongariro is a protected area, so it's important to stick to the trails, take any rubbish with you, and avoid disturbing the natural surroundings. Some parts of the trail, like the Blue Lake, are sacred to the Maori, so please respect the local customs.

5. Arrange Transport

Since the crossing isn't a loop, you'll need to arrange transportation. Many visitors book a shuttle that drops them off at the start and picks them up at the end. This is convenient and ensures you can get back without any hassle.

• **Why Visit Tongariro National Park?**

The Tongariro Alpine Crossing is an incredible journey through one of New Zealand's most amazing landscapes. The volcanic features, colorful lakes, and wide-open views make it a memorable experience. Although it's challenging, the rewards are worth every step, offering hikers a chance to see natural wonders up close and feel the power of New Zealand's active volcanic landscape.

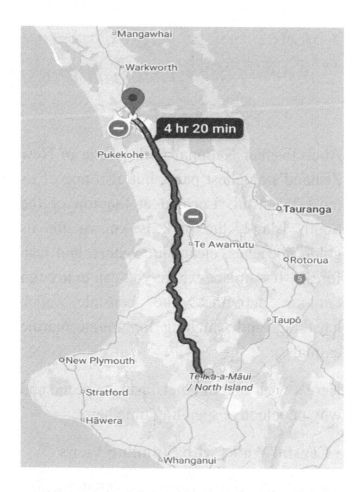

- **The map above shows distance (with time covered) from Auckland to Tongariro National Park**

Coastal walks, kayaking, and marine life (Abel Tasman National Park)

Abel Tasman National Park is one of New Zealand's smallest parks but also one of its most beautiful. Located at the top of the South Island, the park is known for its golden beaches, clear blue waters, and lush forests. It's a place where you can enjoy fun outdoor activities like coastal walks, kayaking, and watching for unique marine animals.

Here's what makes Abel Tasman special and why people love spending time here.

• **Coastal Walks with Stunning Views**

One of the best ways to see Abel Tasman National Park is by walking along the Abel Tasman Coast Track. This is a popular trail that follows the coastline, winding through forests and along sandy beaches. It's about

60 kilometers (around 37 miles) long, so if you wanted to walk the whole thing, it would take about three to five days. But you don't have to walk the whole track; many people just walk a section of it or go for a short day hike.

As you walk along the coast track, you'll see beautiful bays, beaches, and rocky cliffs. You might stop to dip your feet in the water or rest on a quiet beach. Since the track stays close to the water, you'll often get views of the blue ocean and might even see seals or dolphins playing near the shore.

Some highlights along the track include:

- Anchorage Bay

This beach is one of the most popular stops along the track. Anchorage Bay has golden sand and clear, calm water, making it perfect for swimming. You can also camp here if you plan to stay overnight.

- Torrent Bay

Torrent Bay has both a beach and a tidal estuary. If you're there at low tide, you can walk across the sandy estuary, which is fun and gives you a different view of the area.

- Bark Bay

This is a quiet bay surrounded by trees. Many people like to stop here for a picnic or a quick swim in the calm waters.

These are just a few spots, but there are many places along the coast track where you can stop and enjoy the scenery. Since Abel Tasman has plenty of sunshine, it's a pleasant place to walk most of the year.

• Kayaking Adventures in Clear Waters

Kayaking is another great way to explore Abel Tasman. Paddling along the coastline lets you see the park from a different angle, and you can get up close to the water's edge, hidden coves, and small islands. Kayaks allow you to reach places that are hard to get to on foot, giving you a special view of the coastline.

Guided kayak tours are popular, especially for beginners. Experienced guides know the best spots to visit and can help keep you safe. Some tours even take you to places where you're more likely to spot wildlife, like seals or little blue penguins, which are common in the park.

If you feel confident, you can rent a kayak and paddle on your own. Some people like to kayak to a beach and then walk along a section of the Abel Tasman Coast Track before returning. This combination of kayaking and hiking gives you the best of both worlds.

Kayaking in Abel Tasman is especially fun because the water is often calm, making it easier to paddle.

The clear water lets you see fish swimming below you, and you'll get great views of the forested hills along the shore.

• Amazing Marine Life to Discover

One of the things that makes Abel Tasman National Park special is its rich marine life.

Since the park includes both land and sea, it's a great place to see animals both above and below the water.

- Seals

One of the most common marine animals in Abel Tasman is the New Zealand fur seal. These seals like to sunbathe on rocks near the shore and can often be seen splashing in the water.

You might see them when kayaking, or you can visit the seal colony at Tonga Island, which is a protected area where seals gather. Watching seals play or rest is always a highlight.

- Dolphins

If you're lucky, you might spot dolphins swimming in the bay. Dolphins are curious animals, and they sometimes swim close to kayakers or boats, which can be exciting to see. They usually travel in groups, so if you see one dolphin, there might be more nearby.

- Little Blue Penguins

These are the smallest penguins in the world, and you might spot them around Abel Tasman. Little blue penguins are shy and usually come out at dusk or dawn, so they're a bit harder to find. But seeing one waddling along the beach or swimming in the water is a special sight.

- Fish and Other Sea Creatures

The water in Abel Tasman is very clear, so you might see fish swimming near the shore or under your kayak. You can also look out for stingrays, starfish, and crabs along the beach or in shallow water.

If you want to learn more about marine life, there are snorkeling tours available in some areas.

Snorkeling is a fun way to see the fish and underwater plants up close. Some snorkeling spots have rocky reefs where you can see colorful seaweed and small fish swimming among the rocks.

• **Tips for Visiting Abel Tasman National Park**

1. Choose How to Travel

Abel Tasman is accessible by foot, boat, or kayak. Many people like to mix these options by kayaking one way and walking back, or by taking a water taxi to one beach and walking or kayaking from there.

The water taxis are handy and can drop you off at different parts of the park.

2. Bring Sun Protection

The sun can be strong, especially in summer, so wear sunscreen, a hat, and sunglasses to protect yourself. Since much of the walking and kayaking is in the open, you'll need to be prepared.

3. Pack Light but Smart

Bring water, snacks, and a light jacket, as the weather can change quickly. If you're planning to stay overnight, you'll need to carry your camping gear and food.

4. Stay Overnight for More Adventure

Abel Tasman has several campsites and huts along the coast track.

Staying overnight gives you more time to explore and enjoy the peace of the park in the evening and early morning.

You can wake up to the sounds of birds and the gentle waves, making for a relaxing experience.

5. Respect the Environment

Abel Tasman National Park is a protected area, so it's important to stay on trails, pack out all rubbish, and not disturb the wildlife.

The animals and plants here depend on the park being kept clean and undisturbed.

• Why Abel Tasman Is Special

Abel Tasman National Park is special because it combines so many fun activities in one place.

You can hike, kayak, relax on the beach, and see amazing wildlife all in the same day. The mix of clear water, golden beaches, and green forest gives it a cheerful and welcoming feel.

Whether you like walking, paddling, or just sitting and enjoying the view, there's something for everyone here.

People of all ages enjoy Abel Tasman, from kids to adults, because it's easy to explore and offers plenty of choices for how to spend your day.

It's the kind of place that stays in your memory, with its golden sand, playful seals, and peaceful forests, making it a must-see spot on New Zealand's South Island.

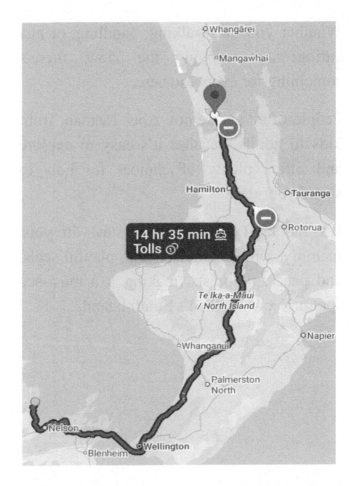

- **The map above shows distance (with time covered) from Auckland to Abel Tasman National Park**

Star-gazing, glacier hikes, and scenic viewpoints (Mount Cook National Park)

Mount Cook National Park is one of New Zealand's most beautiful places, with towering mountains, large glaciers, and wide open skies that seem to go on forever. Known for being home to Mount Cook (Aoraki), the tallest mountain in New Zealand, the park offers a lot of different activities. People come here to hike on glaciers, enjoy clear views of the stars, and take in the amazing scenery.

• Star-Gazing

One of the best things about Mount Cook National Park is the clear night sky. It's located far away from big cities, which means there isn't much light pollution to block out the stars. Because of this, the park is part of the Aoraki Mackenzie

International Dark Sky Reserve, which is a special area protected for its dark, starry skies.

On a clear night, the sky above Mount Cook is filled with thousands of stars. You can see constellations, planets, and even the Milky Way stretching across the sky. If you're lucky, you might even catch a shooting star. For people who live in cities, this is an amazing sight, as it's rare to see so many stars at once.

There are special star-gazing tours you can take, where guides use telescopes to show you details you might miss with just your eyes. These tours help you learn about the stars and planets, making it a fun and educational experience. Some tours are held indoors with special telescopes, so even if it's cold outside, you can still enjoy the view.

If you want to star-gaze on your own, all you need is a warm blanket and a clear spot with an open view of the sky. The best time for star-gazing is during winter, as the sky is usually clearer and the stars shine even brighter.

• Glacier Hikes

Mount Cook National Park is known for its large glaciers, especially the Tasman Glacier, which is the biggest glacier in New Zealand. Glaciers are giant rivers of ice that move slowly down mountains. In Mount Cook, you have the chance to hike on these glaciers or get close enough to see them up close.

The Tasman Glacier is one of the main places people visit. You can take a guided glacier hike, where experienced guides help you safely walk on the ice. These tours usually provide special boots with spikes called crampons, which help you walk without slipping. Walking on the ice is a unique experience – you might see ice caves, deep cracks, and even pools of bright blue water.

If you're not up for hiking on the glacier itself, there are also boat tours that take you across the glacier lake at the bottom of the Tasman Glacier.

These boats bring you close to floating icebergs that have broken off from the glacier. Seeing these large chunks of ice floating in the water is a special sight, and the water's blue color makes it look like something from a movie.

For those who want a closer look but prefer to stay off the ice, there's also the option of taking a helicopter ride.

Helicopter tours offer breathtaking views of the glaciers and let you land on the ice to experience it without a full hike. This way, you get a feel for the glacier's size and beauty from above and up close.

• Scenic Viewpoints

Mount Cook National Park has some of the best scenic viewpoints in New Zealand. The mountains, glaciers, and valleys make the views impressive at any time of year, and there are several places in the park that are perfect for admiring the scenery.

- Hooker Valley Track

This is one of the most popular walking trails in the park. It's an easy hike, and the trail is well-marked, making it suitable for families and beginner hikers.

The track takes you through the Hooker Valley, across swing bridges, and past rivers and glaciers. At the end of the track, you'll reach a glacier lake with views of Mount Cook in the distance.

This spot is especially popular because it's not too hard to reach, yet the views are incredible.

- Kea Point

The Kea Point Track is another shorter trail that gives you excellent views of Mount Cook and the surrounding area. The track takes about an hour, leading you to a viewpoint with a clear look at Mount Cook, the Mueller Glacier, and the mountains around them. It's a great option if you want a shorter walk with rewarding views.

- Tasman Lake Lookout

This viewpoint overlooks Tasman Lake, where the Tasman Glacier ends. From here, you can see the glacier's icy edge and the lake filled with icebergs.

The blue water and chunks of ice create a beautiful scene. This trail is fairly short and offers an easy walk to a lookout that's perfect for photos.

- Mount John Observatory

While it's a bit further from Mount Cook, the Mount John Observatory, located in Lake Tekapo nearby, offers views of the surrounding mountains and lakes as well as star-gazing tours.

During the day, you can see panoramic views of the whole area, and at night, the observatory is one of the best spots for looking at the stars.

• Tips for Visiting Mount Cook National Park

1. Dress for the Weather

The weather in Mount Cook can change quickly, especially in the mountains and near the glaciers. Even in summer, it can be chilly. Make sure to bring warm layers and a waterproof jacket to stay comfortable.

2. Stay Safe on the Trails

Some of the trails in Mount Cook are easy, but others can be more challenging. Make sure to follow marked paths and listen to any advice from park rangers or guides. If you're planning a longer hike, bring enough water and snacks to keep your energy up.

3. Check the Weather Forecast

Since the weather can change quickly, it's a good idea to check the forecast before you start a hike or glacier tour. Some activities, like star-gazing and glacier hikes, are best on clear days, so knowing the weather in advance helps you plan your visit.

4. Bring a Camera

The views in Mount Cook National Park are some of the best in New Zealand, so you'll want to capture them. Bring a camera or phone with enough battery to take photos of the mountains, glaciers, and stars.

5. Respect the Environment

Mount Cook National Park is a protected area, so it's important to keep it clean and follow the park's rules.

• Why Mount Cook National Park Is a Must-Visit

Mount Cook National Park offers an amazing mix of things to do, from watching the stars to hiking on glaciers and enjoying scenic walks. Each season brings a different view, from snow-covered peaks in winter to clear skies in summer, which makes every visit special.

For many people, the combination of Mount Cook's tall mountains, huge glaciers, and endless starry skies creates memories that last a lifetime. Whether you're hiking, stargazing, or just enjoying the views, Mount Cook National Park is a place where nature feels both beautiful and powerful.

- **The map above shows distance (with time covered) from Auckland to Mount Cook National Park**

Chapter Five: Culture and Cuisine

Insights into Maori history, art, and local traditions

New Zealand is also rich in history and culture, thanks to the Maori, the first people to live there. Maori culture is an important part of New Zealand's identity, and learning about it can help us understand the deep connection Maori have with the land, their ancestors, and their unique traditions. Visiting Maori heritage sites, seeing traditional art, and learning about their customs give us a peek into their world.

• **Who Are the Maori?**

The Maori are the indigenous people of New Zealand. They arrived over a thousand years ago from Polynesia, crossing vast oceans in large canoes called "waka." Maori tribes, or "iwi," settled across New Zealand, forming communities with strong bonds and deep respect for nature. They used the land, sea, and forest to gather food, build homes, and develop a lifestyle that was in harmony with their surroundings.

The Maori language, known as "Te Reo Maori," is another key part of their culture.

While English is commonly spoken in New Zealand today, Te Reo is still used, and many people are working hard to keep the language alive by teaching it in schools and using it in everyday life.

• Important Maori Heritage Sites

Visiting Maori heritage sites is a way to connect with their culture and learn about their past.

Here are a few important sites where you can learn about Maori history and their connection to the land.

1. Waitangi Treaty Grounds

Located in the Bay of Islands, the Waitangi Treaty Grounds is a key place in New Zealand's history. This is where, in 1840, Maori chiefs and representatives of the British Crown signed the Treaty of Waitangi, an agreement about land and governance. This treaty is seen as New Zealand's founding document, though its meaning has been interpreted differently over the years.

At the Waitangi Treaty Grounds, visitors can see the "Treaty House," where the document was signed, and explore the "Te Kōngahu Museum," which has exhibits on the treaty, Maori culture, and New Zealand's history. There's also a beautifully carved "wharenui" (meeting house) called "Te Whare

Rūnanga," where you can learn about Maori customs and the significance of these buildings. Outside, you'll find a large "waka" (war canoe) used in traditional ceremonies.

2. Rotorua

Rotorua is known for its geothermal activity, but it's also one of the best places to experience Maori culture up close. The area is home to several Maori villages where people can visit and learn about traditional practices.

- Te Puia

This cultural center in Rotorua is home to the New Zealand Maori Arts and Crafts Institute, where carvers and weavers keep traditional Maori arts alive. You can watch them work, and they'll explain how carving and weaving are passed down through generations. Te Puia is also famous for the

Pohutu Geyser and hot springs, which have special cultural significance.

- Tamaki Maori Village

Here, visitors are welcomed with a "powhiri" (traditional greeting) and can see performances that include "haka" (a powerful war dance), songs, and storytelling. You'll learn about traditional food, especially the "hangi," which is cooked underground using heated stones, a method the Maori have used for centuries.

3. Ohinemutu Village

Ohinemutu is a Maori village located on the shores of Lake Rotorua. It's a living village, which means Maori families still live there today.

This living village is home to the great St. Faith's Church, which blends Maori and Christian art, creating a unique experience.

The church's windows feature images of Christ wearing a Maori cloak, showing the respect between cultures.

Visitors can also see steam rising from natural hot springs around the village, and the locals explain how they use the geothermal energy for cooking and heating. It's a simple but beautiful reminder of how the Maori use natural resources in their daily lives.

4. Tane Mahuta – The Lord of the Forest

In the Waipoua Forest, you'll find Tane Mahuta, the largest and oldest known kauri tree in New Zealand.

Maori legends say Tane Mahuta is the god of the forest, and the tree is named after him. It stands tall and wide, with a massive trunk that's been growing for around 2,000 years.

Seeing Tane Mahuta is a moving experience because of its size and age, and Maori guides often share stories about its importance and the way it connects them to their ancestors.

• Maori Art and Carving

Art and carving are essential to Maori culture. Maori artists often carve wood, stone, and even bone into detailed designs that hold special meanings. Each carving tells a story or represents a concept, like protection, strength, or family ties.

Traditional Maori carvings can be found on "wharenui" (meeting houses), which are gathering places for the community. Every carving in a meeting house has a purpose, whether it's representing ancestors or showing symbols of protection.

Maori weaving is another form of art. Flax, or "harakeke," is woven into baskets, mats, and clothing.

The patterns and methods are passed down from elders, so these crafts connect generations.

• Traditional Maori Customs

Maori customs are based on respect for people, ancestors, and nature. Here are a few important customs that are part of Maori life and culture:

- Powhiri (Welcome Ceremony)

When you visit a Maori village or meeting place, you may experience a powhiri. It's a formal welcome ceremony that includes speeches, songs, and the "hongi," where people press their noses and foreheads together. This is a way of sharing breath and connecting spiritually.

- Haka

The haka is a traditional Maori dance that's well-known around the world, thanks to the New Zealand All Blacks rugby team. It's a way to show pride, strength, and unity. Traditionally, the haka was performed before battles to prepare warriors and show their energy. Today, it's also performed at ceremonies and celebrations.

- Hangi

Maori use the earth to cook food in a method called hangi. Stones are heated in a fire and placed in a pit, then the food, often wrapped in leaves, is put on top and covered. The food slowly cooks, giving it a smoky flavor. A hangi is usually prepared for special occasions, and it's a meal meant to be shared with family and friends.

• Importance of Maori Culture Today

It's an important part of New Zealand's identity and fame. Over the years, Maori have worked to protect their traditions, language, and land. Today, you'll see the Maori language used in schools, government buildings, and public places across New

Zealand. Many young Maori are learning about their heritage, and there are ongoing efforts to make sure Te Reo Maori remains a living language.

Maori culture is respected and celebrated across New Zealand, and it adds to the country's uniqueness. Through art, history, and traditions, the Maori share their way of life with visitors and show us the deep connection they have with their land and ancestors. When people visit Maori heritage sites and join in their customs, they're helping to honor and protect this beautiful culture for generations to come.

Traditional Maori food, local wine regions, and must-try dishes

New Zealand is not just famous for its stunning scenery and rich Maori culture; it also offers some delicious food and drink experiences.

From traditional Maori cooking techniques to some of the world's best wines, New Zealand's food scene is as diverse as its landscapes.

This guide will take you through some of the most interesting dishes, food traditions, and local wines that make New Zealand's cuisine unique and enjoyable.

• Traditional Maori Food

The Maori people have been in New Zealand for hundreds of years, and they've developed unique ways of preparing and cooking food.

Traditional Maori food often uses ingredients found in New Zealand's forests, rivers, and sea. Maori cuisine is based on the idea of "kai," which means food, and it is usually fresh, natural, and cooked in ways that keep the original flavors.

• Hangi

One of the most famous ways Maori people cook food is called the hangi. Hangi is a traditional method where food is cooked in the ground. First, large stones are heated in a fire until they are very hot. Then, the food is wrapped in leaves or cloth, placed in a pit with the hot stones, and covered with soil to trap the heat. The food slowly cooks in this underground oven, creating a smoky, earthy flavor.

Hangi meals often include meats like chicken, lamb, and pork, as well as vegetables such as potatoes, kumara (sweet potatoes), and pumpkin. This cooking method makes the food soft and juicy, and the flavors blend together nicely. Many tourists who visit Maori villages get to try a hangi meal as part of the experience, and it's definitely something not to miss.

• Seafood

New Zealand is surrounded by water, so seafood is an important part of Maori food.

You'll find a variety of fish, along with unique types of shellfish like paua (abalone), kina (sea urchin), and tuatua (a type of clam).

These are often gathered fresh from the sea. Paua, known for its beautiful blue and green shell, is usually served as fritters, where it's minced and mixed with a batter before being fried.

Whitebait fritters are also popular. Whitebait are tiny fish, and in New Zealand, they're mixed with egg and fried into patties.

This dish is very special to locals, and many people look forward to whitebait season every year.

• Rewena Bread

Another traditional Maori food is rewena bread, which is a type of sourdough bread made with potatoes.

The potatoes help make the bread rise, giving it a unique flavor. This bread is soft and slightly sweet, and it's often enjoyed with butter or jam.

Rewena bread is a favorite at gatherings and celebrations and can sometimes be found at farmers' markets or bakeries in New Zealand.

• New Zealand's Wine Regions

New Zealand is known around the world for its excellent wines, and visiting a vineyard is a popular activity.

The country's climate, with cool nights and warm days, is perfect for growing grapes. Here are a few of the main wine regions and the types of wine they are known for.

- **Marlborough**

- **The map above shows distance (with time covered) from Auckland to Marlborough south Island**

The Marlborough region, located at the top of the South Island, is New Zealand's most famous wine area. It's especially known for Sauvignon Blanc, a crisp white wine with flavors of passion fruit, lime, and green apple. Marlborough's Sauvignon Blanc is loved for its fresh, fruity taste, and it's often enjoyed with seafood or salads.

This region also produces other types of wine, like Pinot Noir and Chardonnay, but Sauvignon Blanc is the star. Many vineyards in Marlborough offer tastings, where visitors can sample different wines and learn how they are made.

• Hawke's Bay

Hawke's Bay, located on the North Island, is the second-largest wine-producing region in New Zealand and is known for its rich red wines.

The warm climate here is ideal for grapes used in Merlot, Cabernet Sauvignon, and Syrah. These wines are bold and full of flavor, often with hints of berries, chocolate, and spices.

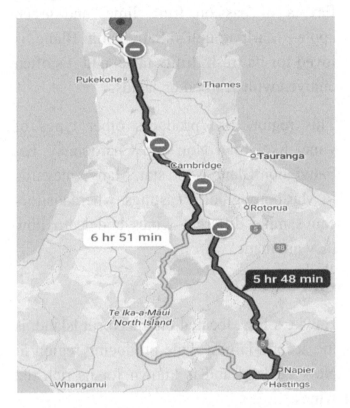

• **The map above shows distance (with time covered) from Auckland to Hawke's Bay**

Hawke's Bay is also known for Chardonnay, a white wine that can be smooth and creamy. Many wineries in this region have lovely views and picnic areas where you can enjoy your wine with a nice meal.

• Central Otago

Central Otago, located on the South Island, is famous for Pinot Noir, a red wine with a light and fruity taste. Pinot Noir grapes are delicate and need just the right climate, which this region provides with its cool temperatures and sunny days.

Central Otago Pinot Noir often has flavors of cherry, plum, and spices, making it popular worldwide. Central Otago is the southernmost wine region in the world, and it's one of the most scenic. The vineyards here are surrounded by mountains, and many of them have tasting rooms where visitors can enjoy the wine along with stunning views.

• **The map above shows distance (with time covered) from Auckland to Central Otago**

• Must-Try New Zealand Dishes

Aside from traditional Maori food, New Zealand has some tasty dishes that visitors should try.

• Fish and Chips

Fish and chips might not be unique to New Zealand, but it's very popular and widely enjoyed. Fresh fish, usually hoki or snapper, is coated in batter and fried until crispy. It's served with chips (fries) and often wrapped in paper. Fish and chips are best eaten at the beach, where you can enjoy the food along with the ocean view.

• Meat Pies

Meat pies are another favorite in New Zealand. These small, hand-sized pies are filled with meat (like beef or lamb), gravy, and sometimes vegetables. There are many flavors, from steak and cheese to mince and onion. Meat pies are warm and filling, making them a great snack or meal on the go.

• **Pavlova**

Pavlova is a dessert that both New Zealand and Australia claim to have invented, and it's a big favorite in New Zealand. This dessert is made from a base of meringue, which is crispy on the outside and soft on the inside. It's topped with whipped cream and fresh fruits like kiwi, strawberries, and passionfruit. Pavlova is light, sweet, and perfect for a summer day.

• **Green-Lipped Mussels**

New Zealand is home to green-lipped mussels, which are larger and have a unique green color on the edge of their shells. These mussels are famous for their health benefits and are often steamed or served in a garlic and wine sauce. Many seafood restaurants along the coast offer fresh green-lipped mussels as a specialty.

• The New Zealand Dining Experience

Eating in New Zealand is a relaxed experience. Many restaurants and cafes are casual, and the focus is often on fresh, local ingredients. Because New Zealand has so much farmland and coastline, many ingredients come straight from local farms and the ocean.

Farmers' markets are also popular, and they're great places to sample local produce, cheeses, and baked goods. You can often find small stalls selling homemade treats and local specialties, like honey from manuka trees or feijoa (a unique fruit grown in New Zealand) products.

Major annual events, including Waitangi Day and regional festivals

New Zealand also has a lively festival and event scene that brings people together from all over. Each year, Kiwis (as New Zealanders are often called) celebrate many important events and festivals. These gatherings celebrate the country's culture, history, and traditions. Here, we'll look at some of the biggest annual events, from national holidays like Waitangi Day to regional festivals that highlight local customs, music, food, and art.

• Waitangi Day

Waitangi Day is one of New Zealand's most important national holidays. It's held every year on February 6 to honor the signing of the Treaty of Waitangi in 1840. The treaty was an agreement between the British

Crown and many Maori chiefs, laying the foundation for New Zealand as a nation. This day is both a time for celebration and reflection, as it brings people together to remember the country's history and the relationship between Maori and Pakeha (non-Maori New Zealanders).

Waitangi Day events are held all over New Zealand, but the main celebration happens at Waitangi Treaty Grounds in the Bay of Islands, where the treaty was originally signed. At Waitangi, there are speeches from leaders, cultural performances, and activities like traditional Maori war canoe (waka) paddling. People enjoy live music, dance performances, and arts and crafts, making it a fun and educational day for all ages.

In other cities, like Auckland and Wellington, there are also festivals, parades, and concerts. For many people, Waitangi Day is a chance to learn more about the history of New Zealand and show respect for Maori culture.

• Matariki

Matariki marks the Maori New Year and is celebrated with the appearance of the Matariki star cluster in the sky, also known as the Pleiades. This usually happens in June or July and signifies a time for new beginnings, remembering those who have passed, and planning for the future.

During Matariki, communities come together to enjoy traditional Maori music, dance, and storytelling. Many families and communities host feasts, known as hakari, and share food as a way to connect and celebrate. There are also Matariki festivals with activities like kite-flying (as kites have special cultural significance), art displays, and star-gazing events.

Matariki is not only a time for fun; it also gives people the chance to connect with nature, set personal goals, and celebrate the unique Maori culture.

• Pasifika Festival

New Zealand has strong connections with the Pacific Islands, and every year, Auckland hosts the Pasifika Festival to celebrate this cultural bond. This festival, held in March, is the largest of its kind in the world, featuring Pacific Island communities like Samoa, Tonga, Fiji, and many more. Pasifika offers a chance to learn about and experience the vibrant cultures, traditions, and foods of the Pacific Islands.

The festival has different "villages" set up to represent each island nation, with food stalls offering traditional dishes, music performances, and cultural displays. Visitors can enjoy lively dances like the Samoan Siva or the Fijian Meke and learn about each culture's unique customs. Pasifika is a bright, colorful festival that brings a taste of the islands to New Zealand and shows the strong connections between these nations.

• World of Wearable Art (WOW)

The World of Wearable Art (WOW) show is one of New Zealand's most unique and creative events. It's held each year in Wellington, usually in September or October, and it combines art, fashion, and theater into one amazing show. WOW challenges designers from around the world to create wild, imaginative costumes that can be worn, but that also push the limits of what "wearable" means.

These wearable art pieces range from clothing made of recycled materials to elaborate costumes that look like they belong in a fantasy world. The show includes lights, music, and dance, making it feel like a big theatrical performance. WOW attracts thousands of visitors and designers from across the globe, making it one of the most exciting events in New Zealand's arts calendar.

• Rhythm and Vines

For music lovers, Rhythm and Vines is the ultimate festival to ring in the New Year. Held in Gisborne, on the North Island, it's known for being the first festival in the world to welcome the new year due to New Zealand's time zone. The event takes place over three days, from December 29 to December 31, and features a variety of music genres, including electronic, pop, hip-hop, and indie.

Rhythm and Vines is set among vineyards, which gives it a unique and beautiful backdrop. Thousands of people from New Zealand and around the world come to dance, camp, and celebrate with friends. It's especially popular with young people, and the lineup often includes well-known international and Kiwi artists.

• Hokitika Wildfoods Festival

The Hokitika Wildfoods Festival, held on the West Coast of the South Island, is perfect for those who want to try something out of the ordinary. This event, usually held in March, is all about unusual food. Here, visitors can sample exotic and quirky dishes like huhu grubs (a type of beetle larvae), wild game, and other "wild" delicacies that you won't find in most restaurants.

The festival isn't just about eating strange foods; it also includes live music, dance, and entertainment. People dress up in costumes, and the event has a playful atmosphere. The Hokitika Wildfoods Festival is great for adventurous eaters and those who want to experience something unique to New Zealand.

• Lantern Festivals

With a large Chinese community in New Zealand, Lantern Festivals are popular events in cities like Auckland and Christchurch to celebrate the Chinese New Year. These festivals take place in late January or February and feature beautiful, colorful lantern displays in the shape of animals, plants, and symbols of Chinese culture.

In addition to lanterns, there are performances such as dragon dances, martial arts, and traditional music. Food stalls offer tasty treats like dumplings, spring rolls, and bubble tea. The Lantern Festival is a lively, family-friendly event that brings people together to celebrate Chinese culture and welcome the New Year.

• **New Zealand International Arts Festival**

The New Zealand International Arts Festival is one of the country's largest arts festivals. Held in Wellington every two years (usually in February and March), it includes theater, music, dance, film, and visual arts from New

Zealand and international artists. The festival attracts performers and visitors from around the world, making it a truly global event.

The arts festival is perfect for people who love cultural performances and want to see high-quality shows. Events take place at various venues around Wellington, from big theaters to small galleries, allowing visitors to experience a wide range of artistic expressions.

• Bluff Oyster and Food Festival

For seafood lovers, the Bluff Oyster and Food Festival is a highlight of the year. Bluff, located at the southern tip of the South Island, is famous for its oysters, considered some of the best in the world. The festival, held in May, celebrates the beginning of oyster season with fresh seafood dishes, including oysters, mussels, and other local seafood treats.

Visitors enjoy live music and entertainment while sampling delicious food. The Bluff Oyster and Food Festival brings people from all over New Zealand and beyond to enjoy this tasty seafood celebration.

Chapter Six: Practical Travel Tips

Overview of hotels, hostels, holiday parks, and unique stays (Accommodation Options)

When you're traveling around New Zealand, finding a good place to stay is important for a comfortable trip.

Luckily, New Zealand offers a wide range of places to suit every budget and style, from hotels and hostels to holiday parks and unique stays that make your visit even more special.

Whether you're looking for a simple bed for the night or a memorable experience in a different kind of setting, New Zealand has plenty of options to explore.

• Hotels

Hotels in New Zealand offer many choices, from luxury spots to simple and affordable rooms.

In the cities, you'll find well-known brands and some charming local hotels that reflect New Zealand's relaxed style.

• **Luxury Hotels**

If you're looking for a luxury experience, consider staying at the **Sofitel Auckland Viaduct Harbour**.

This hotel sits near Auckland's vibrant waterfront, and its rooms offer beautiful views of the marina. In Queenstown, the Eichardt's Private Hotel is another excellent choice. This hotel offers stunning lake views and elegant rooms that make it a favorite for many travelers.

For a unique luxury experience near Rotorua's famous hot springs, the Solitaire Lodge provides a peaceful escape with stunning views over Lake Tarawera. You can even arrange private boat trips and enjoy the natural beauty surrounding the lodge.

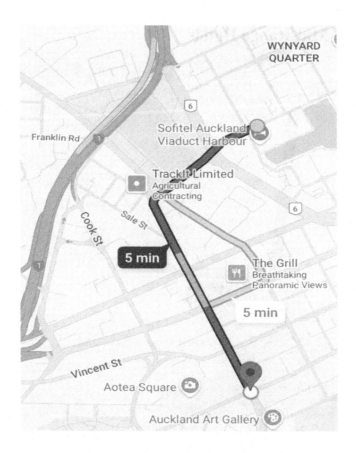

- The map above shows distance (with time covered) from Auckland central to Sofitel Auckland Viaduct Harbour

• Mid-Range Hotels

• **The map above shows distance (with time covered) from Auckland central to Heritage Hotel**

New Zealand also has a good range of mid-range hotels, where you'll find comfort without the high prices of luxury stays. The **Heritage Hotel** in Auckland offers comfortable rooms with a rooftop pool and great city views. In Wellington, Novotel Wellington provides cozy rooms and is located close to the city's main attractions, making it convenient for sightseeing.

For those heading to Christchurch, **Distinction Christchurch Hotel** offers a balance of affordability and quality. The hotel is right near Cathedral Square, so it's easy to get around and enjoy the city's sights.

• The map above shows distance (with time covered) from Auckland to Distinction Christchurch Hotel

• Hostels

Hostels are a popular choice for budget travelers and backpackers, as they're affordable and often have a social atmosphere where you can meet other travelers. Many hostels in New Zealand offer dorm-style rooms, as well as private rooms for those who prefer a bit more privacy.

• Popular Hostels

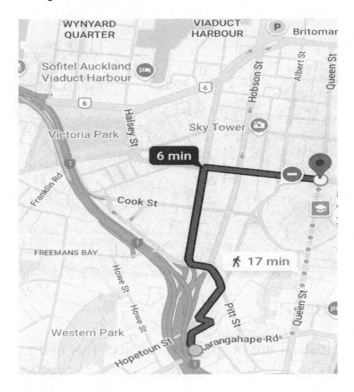

• **The map above shows distance (with time covered) from Auckland central to Haka Lodge**

In Auckland, **Haka Lodge Auckland** is a top pick among backpackers. It's known for its clean rooms and friendly staff, and it's in a convenient location near the city center.

Nomads Queenstown is another popular hostel, offering cozy rooms and a lively atmosphere.

It's also close to Lake Wakatipu, so guests can enjoy beautiful views right from the hostel.

For travelers visiting Wellington, **YHA Wellington** is a well-known hostel offering both dorms and private rooms.

The hostel is eco-friendly, with recycling and sustainable practices, and it's just a short walk from the Te Papa Museum and Wellington's waterfront.

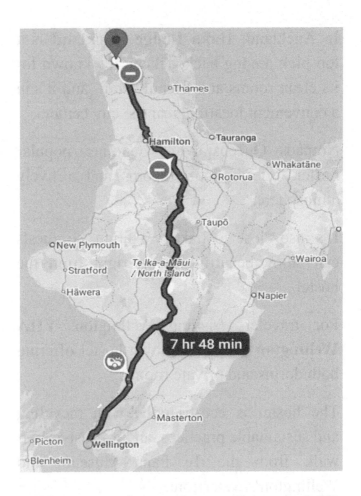

• The map above shows distance (with time covered) from Auckland central to YHA Wellington

• Holiday Parks

Holiday parks are a fantastic choice for families, groups, or anyone who enjoys being close to nature. Holiday parks in New Zealand usually offer a mix of cabins, campsites, and sometimes even self-contained units with kitchens. These parks are often in scenic areas, making them great for travelers who want to explore the outdoors.

• Top Holiday Parks

In Rotorua, the **Blue Lake TOP 10 Holiday Park** is a family-friendly spot with cabins and campsites right by the Blue Lake. The park has plenty of outdoor activities, like kayaking and biking, that keep visitors entertained. Another great option is **Hahei Holiday Resort** on the Coromandel Peninsula, which is close to the famous **Cathedral Cove and Hot Water Beach**.

Guests can camp, stay in cabins, or even rent beachfront villas for a special experience.

On the South Island, Te Anau TOP 10 Holiday Park is an ideal base for exploring Fiordland National Park. The park has a range of accommodation options, from simple cabins to spacious family units, and it's close to activities like hiking and lake cruises.

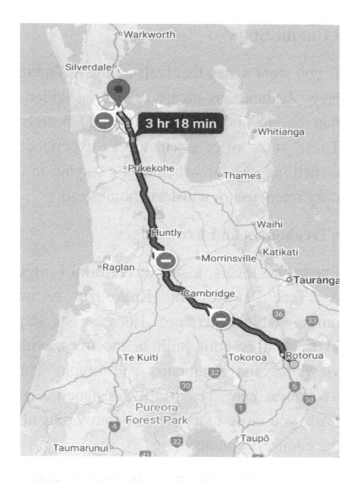

• The map above shows distance (with time covered) from Auckland to Blue Lake TOP 10 Holiday Park

• **Unique Stays**

If you want a stay that feels a little different, New Zealand has plenty of unique options that go beyond typical hotels and hostels. These stays offer a chance to experience something special, whether it's staying in a cozy treehouse or a historic homestead.

• **Treehouses and Eco-Lodges**

For nature lovers, a stay at **Hapuku Lodge & Tree Houses in Kaikoura** is an unforgettable experience. Here, guests stay in treehouses built high in the trees, with views of the mountains and ocean. The treehouses are beautifully designed and bring you close to nature while providing all the comforts you need.

In Golden Bay, The **Boot Bed'n'Breakfast** offers a one-of-a-kind experience. This B&B is shaped like a giant boot, and it's a cozy spot for couples looking for a unique getaway. The hosts make the stay even more enjoyable with their friendly service and home-cooked breakfasts.

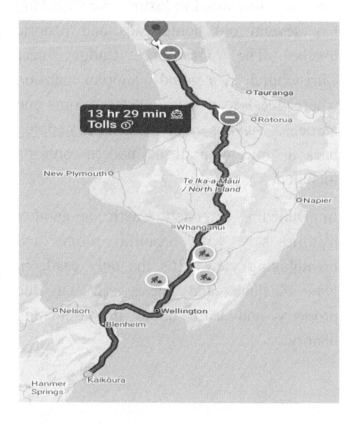

• **The map above shows distance (with time covered) from Auckland to Hapuku Lodge & Tree Houses in Kaikoura**

• Historic Stays

For those interested in history, New Zealand has several old homesteads and historic hotels. The **Otahuna Lodge** near Christchurch is a grand Victorian mansion where guests can enjoy elegant rooms and gardens. Staying here feels like stepping back in time, with all the modern comforts included.

In Dunedin, **Larnach Castle** is another historic stay with beautiful rooms and breathtaking views. It's the only castle in New Zealand, and guests can tour the property and learn about its fascinating history.

• **The map above shows distance (with time covered) from Auckland to Larnach Castle**

• **Farm Stays**

Farm stays are a unique way to experience New Zealand's agricultural side. The Farm at Cape Kidnappers in Hawke's Bay is a luxury farm stay where guests can enjoy comfortable rooms, gourmet meals, and activities like farm tours and golf. The lodge overlooks the ocean, providing stunning views and a peaceful setting.

For a more budget-friendly farm stay, **Tuki Tuki Valley Lodge** near Hastings offers a chance to experience rural life, with cozy rooms and access to vineyards and orchards nearby.

• **Choosing the Right Accommodation for Your Trip**

With so many options, picking the right place to stay depends on your budget, the type of experience you're looking for, and the location you plan to explore.

Whether you're a solo traveler, a family, or a couple, New Zealand's accommodation choices make it easy to find a place that meets your needs.

Each type of accommodation has something unique to offer, so think about what you want most out of your stay.

Do you want a social environment where you can meet other travelers? Or maybe you're hoping to try something a bit out of the ordinary, like a treehouse or a farm stay.

Suggestions for affordable travel, food, and activities

Traveling in New Zealand can be affordable if you know how to plan. With a few smart choices, you can save on food, activities, and accommodation without missing out on the fun.

Here's a guide full of tips and ideas to help you make the most of your time in New Zealand without overspending.

• **Affordable Travel and Transportation**

1. Use Public Transportation

If you're staying in major cities like Auckland or Wellington, take advantage of public transportation.

Buses and trains are often cheaper than renting a car or using taxis. For example, **Auckland Transport (AT)** offers an AT HOP card that gives you discounted rates on buses, trains, and ferries.

2. Look for Ride-Sharing Apps

Ride-sharing apps like **Uber and Ola** can be more affordable than regular taxis in bigger cities.

For longer trips, consider using carpooling services like **BlaBlaCar,** where you can share rides with others going in the same direction. This is not only cost-effective but also a great way to meet new people.

3. Consider Renting a Campervan

If you plan on traveling to multiple towns and cities, renting a campervan can save money on both transportation and accommodation.

Companies like **JUCY and Wicked Campers** offer campervans at affordable rates. With a campervan, you can stay at holiday parks or free camping areas, avoiding the need to pay for hotels.

4. Use Domestic Flights Wisely

Domestic flights can be affordable if booked in advance. Airlines like **Jetstar and Air New Zealand** often have discounted fares, especially for flights between cities like Auckland, Wellington, and Christchurch.

Watch for deals and plan your route to minimize the number of flights.

• **Affordable Food Options**

1. Shop at Local Supermarkets

One of the easiest ways to save on food is by shopping at supermarkets. Stores like **Countdown, Pak'nSave, and New World** have a variety of food options at reasonable prices. If you're staying in accommodation with a kitchen, cooking your own meals can save you a lot of money.

2. Eat at Food Courts and Farmers' Markets

Food courts in cities and malls often offer affordable meals with various choices. In Auckland, **the Ponsonby Central Market** has food stalls where you can try different dishes for a good price. Visiting farmers' markets, like the **Wellington Harbourside Market or the Rotorua Night Market**, is another way to enjoy fresh, local food without overspending.

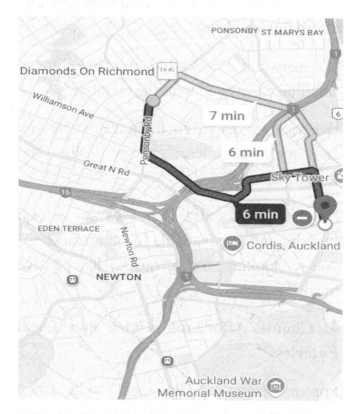

• **The map above shows distance (with time covered) from Auckland central spot to Ponsonby Central Market**

3. Try New Zealand's Classic Takeaways

Takeaway food in New Zealand is typically affordable and tasty.

You can find classics like fish and chips at small takeaways all over the country.

Bakeries are also a good choice, where you can pick up pies, sausage rolls, and sandwiches.

New Zealand's Big Ben Pies are a local favorite and are available in supermarkets if you're looking for a quick, inexpensive meal.

4. Choose Affordable Cafes and Local Eateries

For a budget-friendly meal, skip fancy restaurants and look for local cafes and casual spots.

In Wellington, try **Fidel's Cafe** for affordable coffee and snacks.

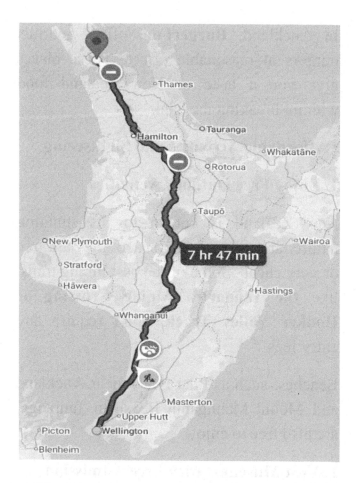

- The map above shows distance (with time covered) from Auckland to Fidel's Cafe

In Auckland, **BurgerFuel** offers gourmet burgers at reasonable prices. These places give you a taste of New Zealand food without breaking the bank.

• **Affordable Activities and Sightseeing**

1. Enjoy Free Outdoor Activities

New Zealand is known for its stunning nature, and many outdoor activities are free or very cheap. Some of the best hiking trails, like **the Tongariro Alpine Crossing or Hooker Valley Track**, don't require any entry fees.

Beaches, such as Piha Beach near Auckland and Mount Maunganui Beach in Tauranga, are also free to enjoy.

2. Visit Museums with Free Admission

Several museums in New Zealand have free admission or donation-based entry.

The Museum of New Zealand Te Papa Tongarewa in Wellington is a fantastic place to learn about the country's history and culture, and it's free to enter.

• **The map above shows distance (with time covered) from Auckland to The Museum of New Zealand Te Papa Tongarewa**

Auckland Art Gallery is also free and showcases a great collection of art.

3. Use i-SITE Visitor Centers for Discounts

i-SITE Visitor Centers, found in many towns and cities across New Zealand, are great places to get discounts on tours, activities, and even accommodation.

The friendly staff can help you find deals and free activities, so it's worth stopping by whenever you reach a new location.

4. Plan Your Own Walking Tours

Instead of booking guided tours, consider planning your own walking tour.

Cities like Auckland, Wellington, and Christchurch have interesting neighborhoods to explore on foot.

In Wellington, a walk along **Cuba Street** lets you enjoy the city's vibrant artsy vibe, while in Christchurch, walking around the Botanic Gardens is a peaceful and free way to experience local beauty.

5. Try Budget-Friendly Wildlife Encounters

You don't have to spend a lot to enjoy New Zealand's unique wildlife.

Willowbank Wildlife Reserve in Christchurch offers affordable tickets to see animals like **kiwis, lemurs, and more**.

In Kaikoura, instead of pricey whale-watching tours, you can sometimes see dolphins and seals along the coast or from affordable, shorter trips.

• Cost-Saving Tips for Accommodation

1. Stay in Hostels

Hostels are a popular budget-friendly accommodation option, especially for solo travelers and backpackers. Many hostels in

New Zealand offer private rooms in addition to dorms. Hostels like **YHA Queenstown Lakefront and Base Backpackers Auckland** are well-rated and provide clean, simple rooms at affordable prices.

2. Choose Holiday Parks and Campgrounds

Holiday parks and campgrounds are great for families and those traveling with campervans. **Top 10 Holiday Parks** have locations across New Zealand and offer a range of options, from tent sites to cabins. These parks usually have shared kitchen facilities, helping you save on meals as well.

3. Book Airbnb or Budget Motels

Airbnb offers budget options in various areas, letting you stay in local homes and sometimes access kitchens to cook your meals. Motels, like **Bella Vista Motel and Econo Lodge Napier**, provide affordable rooms with basic amenities, making them good choices for budget-conscious travelers.

4. Look for Deals and Off-Season Rates

New Zealand has different travel seasons, with peak times in summer and winter. Shoulder seasons are periods to save money. So, consider visiting at that time. Accommodation and activity rates are usually lower, and popular spots are less crowded. Check websites like Booking dot com and Expedia for discounts, and book in advance to secure the best deals.

• Smart Spending Tips to Keep Your Budget in Check

1. Use a Travel Card with No Foreign Transaction Fees

Using a travel card with no foreign transaction fees can save you money when paying for things in New Zealand. Cards like **the Wise Multi-Currency Card or**

Revolut offer good exchange rates and can help you avoid extra fees.

2. Stay Updated on Local Deals and Vouchers

Some websites and apps provide discounts and vouchers for meals, activities, and shopping. Sites like **GrabOne and BookMe** often have deals for attractions, restaurant meals, and tours. Checking these before you make plans can help you find great discounts.

3. Plan for Unexpected Expenses

While budgeting, remember to set aside a bit for unexpected costs. Whether it's an extra fee for luggage or a small splurge on a fun activity, having a buffer in your budget ensures you won't run short on funds during your trip.

Essentials for outdoor travel, climate-specific packing advice, and health tips

When you're getting ready for an outdoor adventure in New Zealand, knowing what to pack is very important. The country has a variety of climates and weather conditions, so packing wisely can make your trip more enjoyable. Here's a helpful guide to ensure you have everything you need for your travels, along with some health tips to keep you safe and happy.

• **Essentials for Outdoor Travel**

1. Clothing Layers

One of the best ways to stay comfortable while hiking or exploring is to wear layers. This means wearing several types of clothing that you can add or remove depending on the weather. Start with a moisture-wicking base layer, like a T-shirt made from merino wool or synthetic fabric, which helps keep sweat away from your skin. Brands like Icebreaker and Kathmandu offer good options.

Next, wear an insulating layer, like a fleece or a light sweater, to keep you warm. Finally, finish off with a waterproof and windproof outer layer, such as a rain jacket or a lightweight shell. Look for jackets from brands like The North Face or Columbia, which are known for their quality outdoor gear.

2. Comfortable Footwear

Your feet are going to be doing a lot of walking, so it's crucial to have the right shoes. Hiking boots or sturdy trail shoes with good grip will help keep you safe and comfortable on rocky or uneven terrain. Brands like **Merrell and Salomon** have well-reviewed options that are perfect for New Zealand's trails. Don't forget to break in your shoes before your trip to avoid blisters!

3. Backpack

This is important in carrying your gear. Look for one that fits comfortably and has enough space for your essentials, like food, water, and extra clothing. Daypacks from companies like **Osprey and Deuter** are excellent choices for day hikes. Aim for a pack that has padded straps and a breathable back to keep you comfortable during long walks.

4. Hydration Gear

Staying hydrated is important, especially during outdoor activities. Bring a reusable water bottle, or consider a hydration bladder that fits inside your backpack. CamelBak makes popular hydration systems that are easy to use while on the go. Make sure to fill your water bottle before starting your hikes, as water sources can be scarce in some areas.

• **Climate-Specific Packing Advice**

1. Coastal Areas

If you're visiting coastal areas like Abel Tasman National Park, be prepared for a mix of sun and rain. Pack lightweight, breathable clothing, a swimsuit for swimming, and a sun hat. Don't forget sunscreen with a high SPF to protect your skin from UV rays. Sunglasses are also a good idea.

2. Mountain Regions

In places like Mount Cook National Park, temperatures can drop quickly, even in summer. Bring warm clothing, including a beanie and gloves, and layer up with thermal tops and bottoms. A good pair of thermal socks will keep your feet warm during chilly hikes. Don't forget your camera to capture the stunning views!

3. The Fiordland Region

Fiordland can be rainy, so waterproof clothing is a must. A good pair of waterproof pants will keep you dry, even during unexpected downpours. Also, pack quick-drying clothes, as you may encounter wet conditions. Waterproof bags for your electronics, like your phone or camera, are also a smart choice.

4. The North Island

In areas like Rotorua, where geothermal activity creates a humid climate, lightweight clothing is essential. Bring a light jacket for cooler evenings. Also, pack sturdy sandals for relaxing in hot pools or walking around the volcanic landscape.

• Health Tips for Outdoor Travelers

1. Stay Active and Stretch

Before and during your trip, make sure to stay active. Stretching helps keep your muscles warm and flexible, especially if you plan to hike for long periods. Simple stretches for your legs and back can prevent stiffness and injury. If you're not used to hiking, consider taking short walks before your trip to prepare your body.

2. Use Insect Repellent

In some parts of New Zealand, especially in warmer months, mosquitoes can be a nuisance. Packing insect repellent will help keep them away. Look for products that contain DEET or natural alternatives like **Citronella**. Don't forget to apply it before you head into areas where insects are common, like forests or near water.

3. Sun Safety

The sun in New Zealand can be very strong, even on cloudy days. Always apply sunscreen with a high SPF to all exposed skin before going outdoors. Wearing a wide-brimmed hat and long-sleeved shirts can provide extra protection against the sun's rays.

4. Be Prepared for Changes in Weather

Weather in New Zealand can change quickly, especially in the mountains. Always check the forecast before heading out and be prepared for different conditions. Bring a small emergency kit that includes a first aid kit, a whistle, and a flashlight. Packing a map or a GPS device can help you stay on track.

5. Know Your Limits

It's important to listen to your body and know when to take a break. If you feel tired or unwell, find a safe spot to rest. Drink water frequently to stay hydrated, and don't push yourself too hard on challenging hikes.

Chapter Seven: Seven-Day Itinerary for New Zealand

Day 1: Auckland

Welcome to New Zealand! Your adventure starts in Auckland, the largest city in the country. It is a vibrant city with beautiful parks, stunning harbors, and a mix of cultures. On your first day, you will discover the sights and sounds of Auckland. Let's plan an exciting day that will give you a taste of everything this city has to offer!

• **Morning**

Start your day by arriving at Auckland Airport. After landing, make your way to your accommodation to drop off your bags. There are many places to stay in Auckland, such as **SkyCity Hotel**, which is in the heart of the city, or **Auckland City Hotel**, offering cozy rooms and great service.

• **The map above shows distance (with time covered) from Auckland central spot to SkyCity Hotel**

Once you've settled in, it's time for breakfast. A popular spot for a delicious morning meal is **Federal Delicatessen**. This café offers tasty options like pancakes, eggs benedict, and fresh coffee. Try their bagels with cream cheese; they are a hit among locals and visitors alike!

• **Mid-Morning**

After breakfast, make your way to the **Auckland Sky Tower**. Standing at 328 meters tall, it is the tallest structure in New Zealand. Take the elevator up to the observation deck, where you can enjoy breathtaking views of the city and the surrounding landscapes. On a clear day, you can see the sparkling waters of the Waitemata Harbour, the distant islands, and the rolling hills.

While you're up there, look for the glass floor where you can see straight down to the ground below. It's a fun way to feel like you're floating in the air! The Sky Tower also offers a thrilling activity called the

SkyJump, where you can jump off the tower while being safely harnessed. If you're feeling brave, it could be a great way to start your adventure!

• **Afternoon**

After your visit to the Sky Tower, head to the **Auckland Waterfront.** This area is lively and filled with cafes, shops, and parks. Take a leisurely stroll along the **Viaduct Harbour**, where you can watch boats sailing in and out.

There are often street performers and artists showcasing their talents, making it a fun place to explore.

When you get hungry, stop for lunch at **Harbourside Ocean Bar Grill**, known for its fresh seafood. Their fish and chips are popular, and you can enjoy a beautiful view of the harbor while you eat.

If you're feeling adventurous, try some local dishes like paua (abalone) or whitebait fritters.

• **The map above shows distance (with time covered) from Auckland central spot to Harbourside Ocean Bar Grill**

• Late Afternoon

After lunch, make your way to the **Auckland War Memorial Museum** in **Auckland Domain**, one of the city's oldest parks.

The museum has fascinating exhibits about New Zealand's history, including its natural history, Maori culture, and military history. As you walk through the museum, look for the stunning Maori artifacts and the impressive bone carving displays.

One of the highlights is the giant moa skeleton, which showcases New Zealand's unique wildlife. The museum also has a lovely garden where you can relax and take in the fresh air.

• Evening

As the sun starts to set, head to Ponsonby, a trendy neighborhood known for its cafes, shops, and vibrant nightlife. The streets are lined with colorful Victorian houses, and it's a great place to walk around and enjoy the atmosphere.

• **The map above shows distance (with time covered) from Auckland central spot to Mamak Malaysian Restaurant**

For dinner, visit **Mamak Malaysian Restaurant** for some delicious Malaysian food. Their roti canai (a flaky flatbread) and chicken satay are must-tries! If you prefer a different flavor, check out **Pasta e Vino**, which offers tasty Italian dishes made with fresh ingredients.

• **Night**

After a busy day, return to your accommodation to unwind. If you're staying at **SkyCity Hotel**, you can enjoy a drink at The Sky Lounge, which offers beautiful views of the city skyline at night. It's the perfect way to reflect on your first day in New Zealand.

Day 2: Bay of Islands

On the second day of your New Zealand adventure, you will visit the beautiful Bay of Islands. This area is famous for its stunning beaches, clear blue waters, and rich history.

The Bay of Islands is made up of over 140 islands, making it a perfect spot for outdoor activities and fun experiences. Get ready for a day full of excitement and exploration!

• Morning

Start your day early by having breakfast at your accommodation in Auckland. If you're staying at the **SkyCity Hotel**, enjoy their buffet breakfast with a variety of options to fuel up for the day. After breakfast, it's time to head to the Bay of Islands, which is about a three-hour drive from Auckland.

If you have a rental car, the drive will be scenic, with lush green hills and beautiful landscapes along the way. If you prefer not to drive, you can take a bus or join a guided tour, which might include interesting stops along the route.

• Arriving at Paihia

Once you arrive, you will most likely start your adventure in **Paihia**, a charming town and one of the main gateways to the Bay of Islands. After parking or getting off the bus, take a moment to enjoy the stunning views of the bay. The water is a brilliant shade of blue, and the islands in the distance look like little gems scattered across the sea.

• Mid-Morning

After soaking in the views, your first stop should be the **Waitangi Treaty Grounds**.

This is an important historical site where the Treaty of Waitangi was signed in 1840 between the British and the Māori chiefs. The grounds are home to a museum, a traditional Māori meeting house, and beautiful gardens.

Join a guided tour to learn about the history and significance of the treaty. You'll see a large Māori war canoe, which is impressive to look at!

The tour guides are friendly and will share interesting stories about New Zealand's past. Don't forget to take lots of pictures, especially in the beautiful gardens with views of the bay.

• **Afternoon**

After exploring Waitangi, head back to Paihia and hop on a boat for a cruise around the Bay of Islands.

There are many options, but a popular choice is the **Fullers GreatSights Cruise**, which takes you to see some of the best spots in the bay.

The boat ride is a fantastic way to see the islands, and you might even spot dolphins swimming alongside!

During the cruise, you will stop at some of the beautiful islands. One of the highlights is **Roberton Island**, where you can go for a short walk and enjoy a picnic.

The sandy beaches are perfect for a swim, and the water is usually warm and inviting.

• Late Afternoon

After your cruise, take a short ferry ride from **Paihia to Russell**, a historic town that was once the first capital of New Zealand. Russell is known for its charming streets, old buildings, and beautiful waterfront. Once you arrive, spend some time walking around the town.

Make sure to visit **Christ Church**, which is one of the oldest churches in New Zealand.

It has a unique history and beautiful architecture. After that, you can stop by the **Russell Museum** to learn more about the area's history, including the whaling industry and the early Māori settlers.

If you're feeling hungry, grab a bite to eat at **Duke of Marlborough Hotel**. They have a lovely outdoor area with views of the bay.

Try their famous fish and chips, or if you want to try something local, go for the green-lipped mussels.

• **Evening**

After exploring Russell, take the ferry back to Paihia and enjoy a relaxing evening. You can stroll along the waterfront, where you will find cafes and ice cream shops. Treat yourself to a scoop of delicious ice cream at Dairy Flat, a local favorite known for its tasty flavors.

If you're up for some evening fun, consider joining a sunset cruise. This is a beautiful way to end the day, watching the sun dip below the horizon while enjoying the gentle waves of the bay.

Day 3: Rotorua

On the third day of your New Zealand adventure, you will visit Rotorua, a unique city known for its stunning geothermal activity and rich Māori culture. This place is filled with bubbling mud pools, steaming geysers, and beautiful lakes. You will also experience the warmth and hospitality of the Māori people, making your visit truly special. Get ready for a day packed with fun activities and learning!

• **Morning**

Start your day with a hearty breakfast at your accommodation. If you're staying at the **Novotel Rotorua Lakeside**, you can enjoy a delicious meal with a view of Lake Rotorua. After breakfast, it's time to head to Rotorua, which is about a three-hour drive from the Bay of Islands. If you're not driving, you can take a bus, which will allow you to relax and enjoy the scenery.

Once you arrive in Rotorua, you will immediately notice the unique smell of sulfur in the air. This is a sign of the geothermal activity that makes Rotorua so famous. Your first stop will be **Te Puia**, a geothermal park that showcases the best of the area's natural wonders.

• Late Morning

At Te Puia, you can see geysers, hot springs, and bubbling mud pools up close. The park is home to the famous **Pohutu Geyser**, which shoots water high into the air, sometimes reaching 30 meters.

Make sure to check the schedule to see when the geyser is expected to erupt. You might get lucky and witness it!

While at Te Puia, you will also learn about Māori culture. The park is home to a carving school where students create beautiful wooden carvings using traditional techniques.

You can watch the artists at work and even try your hand at some carving. It's a great way to understand the importance of art in Māori culture.

• Afternoon

After exploring Te Puia, it's time for lunch. Head over to **The Redwoods Treewalk**, where you can enjoy a meal at the **Redwoods Café**. The café offers a variety of tasty options, including fresh sandwiches and delicious cakes. Enjoy your meal while surrounded by the towering trees of the redwood forest.

After lunch, get ready for a special experience: a traditional Māori hāngī feast. A hāngī is a method of cooking food using heated rocks buried in the ground. It is a significant part of Māori culture and is often served during cultural performances.

You can join a hāngī experience at places like **Tamaki Māori Village**. Here, you will learn how the food is prepared and have the chance to participate in traditional ceremonies. After the cooking is done, you'll enjoy a delicious meal featuring meats, vegetables, and sweet desserts. The food is cooked to perfection and has a unique smoky flavor.

• Evening

After enjoying your hāngī feast, the evening will feature an exciting cultural performance. You will see traditional Māori dances, including the haka, which is a powerful and energetic dance often performed to show strength and unity. The performers wear traditional clothing and share stories about their ancestors and culture. It's a fun and educational experience that gives you a deeper understanding of Māori traditions.

• Late Evening

After a day filled with activities, you might want to relax and unwind. Head to the **Polynesian Spa**, one of the best hot spring spas in New Zealand. The spa has several thermal pools with natural minerals that are great for your skin and overall well-being.

Choose a pool with a view of Lake Rotorua and soak in the warm water while gazing at the stars above. This is a perfect way to end your busy day. If you're feeling adventurous, try the **Lake Spa** area, where you can enjoy a luxurious mud wrap or a massage.

Day 4: Waitomo Caves and Hobbiton

On your fourth day in New Zealand, you will visit two amazing places: the **Waitomo Caves and Hobbiton**. This day is going to be filled with adventure, magic, and a little bit of movie magic too!

From exploring stunning underground caves to stepping into the world of **The Lord of the Rings**, you will have a day to remember.

• Morning

Start your day with breakfast at your hotel. If you are staying at **Rydges Rotorua**, they offer a delicious buffet with lots of choices, including pancakes, eggs, and fresh fruits. After breakfast, it's time to hit the road to Waitomo Caves, which is about a two-hour drive from Rotorua.

The journey to Waitomo is beautiful, with rolling hills and lush green fields. You might even spot some sheep grazing along the way, as New Zealand is famous for its sheep farms. When you arrive at Waitomo, you will be greeted by the entrance to the caves, a place where nature shows off its amazing creations.

• Late Morning

Once you arrive at Waitomo, you can start your adventure inside the caves. **The Waitomo Glowworm Caves** are famous for their tiny glowworms that light up the dark caves like stars in the night sky. You can join a guided tour, which lasts about an hour. The tour guide will tell you all about the history of the caves and how glowworms live.

As you walk through the cave, you will see beautiful rock formations, stalactites, and stalagmites that have formed over thousands of years. The highlight of the tour is when you take a small boat ride through the cave, surrounded by glowing lights. It feels like you are floating through a magical underground world.

• Afternoon

After your cave adventure, it's time to refuel with lunch. You can visit **The Waitomo Homestead**, which offers a cozy atmosphere and a menu with delicious options like burgers, sandwiches, and fresh salads. Enjoy your meal while sharing stories about your cave experience with your friends or family.

Once you're finished with lunch, it's just a short drive to Hobbiton, located in the picturesque Waikato region. The journey takes about 30 minutes, and as you travel, you will see beautiful farmland and rolling hills.

• **Early Afternoon**

Hobbiton is a real-life movie set from **The Lord of the Rings and The Hobbit.** When you arrive, you will feel like you have stepped into a storybook. You can take a guided tour that lasts about two hours. During the tour, a friendly guide will lead you through the charming village of Hobbiton, sharing fun facts about the movies and the making of the set.

As you walk around, you will see the colorful hobbit holes, lush gardens, and the famous **Green Dragon Inn**. You can even stop for a refreshing drink at the inn, trying some special brews made just for Hobbiton visitors. Don't forget to take plenty of photos; this place is picture-perfect!

• **Late Afternoon**

One of the coolest things about Hobbiton is getting up close to the hobbit holes. Each hole is unique, with different colors and decorations. Some of them even have little vegetable gardens in front. You can imagine what it would be like to live in a cozy hobbit hole, surrounded by nature and good friends.

Another fun stop on the tour is the **Party Tree**, which is a large tree where Bilbo's birthday party took place in the movies. Standing under this beautiful tree, you can really feel the magic of the story.

• **Evening**

As your visit to Hobbiton comes to an end, you can enjoy a delightful dinner at **The Green Dragon Inn**. They offer a Hobbit Feast, which is a hearty meal featuring traditional dishes like roasted meats, fresh vegetables, and mouthwatering desserts. Eating in this iconic setting will feel like a true Hobbit experience.

Day 5: Queenstown

On your fifth day in New Zealand, you will travel to Queenstown, known as the adventure capital of the country. This beautiful town is surrounded by stunning mountains and a crystal-clear lake, making it a perfect place for outdoor fun. Whether you like thrilling activities or just want to enjoy the scenery, Queenstown has something for you.

• Morning

Start your day with breakfast at your hotel. If you are staying at the **Novotel Queenstown Lakeside**, you can enjoy a delicious buffet with fresh fruits, pastries, and hot options like eggs and bacon. After breakfast, it's time to pack your bags and head out. If you're driving from Rotorua, the trip to Queenstown will take about six hours, but you can break up the drive with a few stops along the way.

As you travel, the landscape will change from rolling hills to dramatic mountains. Keep your camera ready because the views will be amazing! You will see lush green valleys, towering peaks, and perhaps even a few lakes along the route.

• **Late Morning**

When you arrive in Queenstown, your first stop should be the **Remarkables**, a stunning mountain range just outside the town. You can take the **Remarkables Road** for a scenic drive, stopping at lookout points to take in the breathtaking views. If you are feeling adventurous, consider taking a short hike along one of the trails. The views of the surrounding mountains and Lake Wakatipu are simply beautiful.

• Afternoon

After taking views of the place, it's time to have some fun and exercise! Queenstown is famous for its adventure activities. You can choose from a variety of exciting options:

1. Bungee Jumping

If you are feeling brave, try bungee jumping off the Kawarau Bridge. It's the world's first commercial bungee jumping site, and the experience is thrilling as you leap off the bridge and bounce above the river below.

2. Jet Boating

For an adrenaline rush on the water, hop on a jet boat with **Shotover Jet**.

These fast boats zoom through the narrow canyons of the **Shotover River**, twisting and turning at high speeds.

Hold on tight as you experience the excitement of 360-degree spins!

3. Skyline Gondola

If you prefer a more relaxed activity, take the **Skyline Gondola** to the top of **Bob's Peak**.

The ride offers stunning views of Queenstown and the surrounding mountains. Once at the top, you can enjoy lunch at the **Stratosfare Restaurant**, which has an incredible view over the town.

• Late Afternoon

After your thrilling adventures, take some time to relax by **Lake Wakatipu**. This beautiful lake is perfect for a stroll along its shore.

You can also rent a kayak or paddleboard from places like **Queenstown Kayak Tours** and enjoy some time on the water. Keep an eye out for local wildlife, as you might spot ducks and other birds enjoying the lake too.

• **Evening**

As the sun begins to set, it's time for dinner. For a taste of New Zealand cuisine, you can visit **Fergburger**, a famous burger joint that many people rave about. Their burgers are huge and delicious, with options like the **"Ferg Classic" or "Big Al."** Don't forget to try their homemade sauces!

After dinner, take a stroll through the town center. Queenstown has a lively atmosphere with shops, cafes, and street performers. You can also visit the **Queenstown Gardens**, where you can walk through beautiful gardens and even play a game of frisbee golf.

Day 6: Milford Sound

On your sixth day in New Zealand, get ready to visit one of the most beautiful places in the world: **Milford Sound**. This stunning fiord is known for its towering cliffs, cascading waterfalls, and amazing wildlife. Whether you're cruising on the water, hiking along the trails, or simply taking in the views, Milford Sound is sure to leave you speechless. Let's get started on this exciting adventure!

• **Early Morning**

Start your day early with breakfast at your accommodation. If you stay at the **Hilton Queenstown Resort & Spa,** you can enjoy a hearty breakfast with fresh fruit, pancakes, and eggs to fuel you for the day ahead. After breakfast, it's time to hit the road to Milford Sound.

The scenery along the way is incredible, so keep your camera handy! You will pass through **Te Anau**, a charming town where you can stop for a quick snack or pick up supplies. From Te Anau, the road leads into

Fiordland National Park, where the views become even more spectacular.

As you drive, be on the lookout for **Mirror Lakes**, where the mountains reflect beautifully on the water. There are also plenty of spots to stop and take pictures of the lush rainforest and mountains.

• **Late Morning**

When you arrive at Milford Sound, you'll be greeted by breathtaking views of towering cliffs and stunning waterfalls. One of the first things you should do is hop on a boat cruise to really experience the beauty of the fiord. Companies like **Real Journeys and Mitre Peak Cruises** offer amazing tours that last about two hours.

During the cruise, you'll see famous landmarks like **Mitre Peak**, which rises almost 1,700 meters straight up from the water. Look out for **Bowen Falls**, one of the tallest waterfalls in the area, and keep an eye out for wildlife. You might see dolphins swimming alongside the boat, seals resting on the rocks, and even the occasional penguin!

• **Afternoon**

After your boat cruise, if you're up for more adventure, consider going kayaking in Milford Sound.

Milford Sound Kayak offers guided tours where you can paddle through the calm waters and get a closer look at the scenery.

This is a great way to enjoy the peacefulness of the fiord and see the cliffs from a different angle.

While kayaking, you can hear the sounds of nature all around you. The only thing you might hear is the splash of your paddle and the gentle lapping of the water against your kayak.

It's a fantastic way to connect with the environment and appreciate the beauty of Milford Sound.

• **Late Afternoon**

After kayaking, take some time to explore the area on foot. There are several walking tracks around Milford Sound that offer stunning views.

One popular walk is the **Milford Foreshore Walk**, which takes you along the water's edge and offers great views of the cliffs and mountains.

It's an easy walk, perfect for families, and it usually takes about 30 minutes.

If you're looking for something a bit more challenging, you can hike the **Mackinnon Track**, which is part of the larger **Routeburn Track**.

This hike takes you through lush rainforest and offers spectacular views of the mountains and valleys.

• Evening

As the day winds down, it's time to head back to Queenstown. The drive back will be just as beautiful as the drive in, so take your time and enjoy the scenery. If you want, you can stop for dinner in **Te Anau** before continuing on your journey. The Fat Duck is a great place to grab a meal, offering a variety of tasty dishes that include local favorites.

Once you return to Queenstown, you might want to relax and reflect on your incredible day. If you still have energy, take a stroll along Lake Wakatipu. The lake looks different at night, with the stars reflecting on the water.

Day 7: Wanaka

On your final day in New Zealand, you'll explore the charming town of **Wanaka**, known for its stunning lake and majestic mountains. Wanaka is the perfect place to relax and soak up the beautiful scenery after an adventurous week. From outdoor activities to delicious food, there's plenty to enjoy.

Let's dive into your exciting day in Wanaka!

• Early Morning

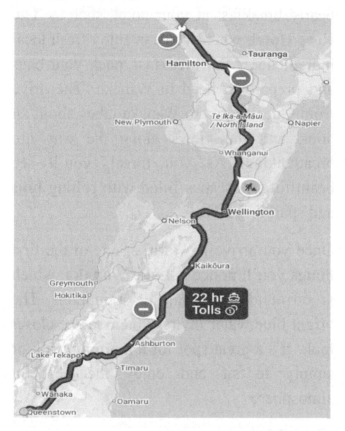

• **The map above shows distance (with time covered) from Auckland to The Rees Hotel**

After a restful night in Queenstown, have a hearty breakfast at your hotel, such as **The Rees Hotel**, where you can enjoy fresh local ingredients. After breakfast, pack your bags and prepare to head to Wanaka. The drive from Queenstown to Wanaka takes about an hour, and the views along the way are breathtaking. As you travel, you'll see beautiful landscapes filled with rolling hills and sparkling lakes.

Once you arrive in Wanaka, one of the first things you'll notice is **Lake Wanaka**, which is surrounded by majestic mountains. The bright blue water invites you to take a closer look. It's a great spot for a morning walk or simply to sit and enjoy the peaceful atmosphere.

• Late Morning

After taking in the beautiful scenery at the lake, take some time to explore the town of Wanaka. The main street is filled with charming shops, cafes, and art galleries. You can stop by Wanaka's famous **'That Wanaka Tree'**, a lone tree that stands in the water and is one of the most photographed spots in New Zealand.

If you're interested in art, visit the **Wanaka Fine Art Gallery**, which showcases a variety of local and national artists. The artwork often reflects the stunning landscapes of the area.

• **Lunch**

After exploring, it's time for lunch. Wanaka has many great places to eat. Consider heading to **Big Fig**, known for its delicious slow-cooked meals and fresh salads.

You can enjoy a hearty meal that will keep you energized for the rest of the day.

If you're in the mood for something sweet, don't miss out on the famous **Wanaka Candy Shop**.

They offer a wide range of tasty treats, from handmade chocolates to gummies that will delight your taste buds!

• **Afternoon**

After lunch, it's time for some outdoor fun! Wanaka offers a variety of activities, whether you're looking for something relaxing or more adventurous. Here are a couple of options:

1. Hiking

If you love nature, consider hiking to **Mount Iron**. This track takes about 1.5 hours to reach the summit, and the views from the top are amazing. You'll see the whole town of Wanaka, Lake Wanaka, and the surrounding mountains.

2. Biking

Another great option is to rent a bike and explore the scenic **Lake Wanaka Loop**. This flat, easy ride allows you to enjoy the beautiful lakeside views while getting some exercise. You can rent bikes from local shops like **Wanaka Bike Tours.**

3. Water Sports

If you're feeling adventurous, why not try paddleboarding or kayaking on Lake Wanaka?

Paddle Wanaka offers rentals and lessons for all skill levels. Gliding across the water while surrounded by mountains is an unforgettable experience.

• Late Afternoon

After your outdoor adventure, take some time to relax by the lake. You can find a peaceful spot to sit down, breathe in the fresh air, and enjoy the view.

If you have time, consider visiting **Rippon Vineyard**, where you can taste some local wines while enjoying stunning views of the lake and mountains.

• Evening

As the sun begins to set, head to one of Wanaka's lovely restaurants for dinner. **Kika** is a fantastic choice, offering delicious dishes made from fresh local ingredients. Try their seasonal specials or a classic burger—it's sure to be a satisfying end to your day.

After dinner, take a stroll along the lakeside path. The colors of the sunset reflecting on the water create a magical scene. This is a wonderful moment to reflect on your amazing week in New Zealand and all the incredible experiences you've had.

OTHER BOOKS RECOMMENDATION

Dear Reader,

If you liked this guide, **Jude** suggests checking out for his other books you might want to add to your reading list.

Thank you for being a valued reader! He looks forward to accompanying you on many more literary journeys.

A KIND GESTURE

Dear Fellow Travelers,

Your feedback on the guide is important to **Jude**. If it made your **trip** more magical, he'd appreciate it if you left a review and shared your experience with others. By spreading the word, you'll help fellow travelers have amazing adventures too.
Thank you for being part of this community of great adventurers. Your kind gesture in leaving a review and recommending the guide is a meaningful contribution to the shared joy of exploration.

Safe travels and happy exploring!
Jude K. Bremner

TRAVEL NOTE

TRAVEL NOTE

TRAVEL NOTE

TRAVEL NOTE

TRAVEL NOTE

TRAVEL NOTE

TRAVEL NOTE

TRAVEL NOTE

_____

_____

_____

_____

_____

_____

_____

_____

_____

_____

_____

TRAVEL NOTE

TRAVEL NOTE

_____

_____

_____

_____

_____

_____

_____

_____

_____

_____

_____

_____

Made in United States
North Haven, CT
20 December 2024

63111300R00173